A Simple

Excel 97

L. Steven

Prentice Hall Europe

London New York Toronto Sydney Tokyo Singapore Madrid
Mexico City Munich Paris

First published in 1997 as Excel 97 – Se Former en 1 Jour by
Simon & Schuster Macmillan (France)
This edition published 1999 by
Prentice Hall Europe
Campus 400, Maylands Avenue
Hemel Hempstead
Hertfordshire, HP2 7EZ

A division of
Simon & Schuster International Group

© 1997 Simon & Schuster Macmillan (France)
19, rue Michel Le Comte
75003 Paris
France

Translated by Berlitz Translation Services UK, Baldock, Hertfordshire

Printed and bound in Great Britain by
Redwood Books, Trowbridge, Wiltshire

Library of Congress Cataloging-in-Publication Data

Available from the publisher

British Library Cataloguing in Publication Data

A catalogue record for this book is available from the British Library
ISBN 0-13-012194-0

1 2 3 4 5 03 02 01 00 99

Table of Contents

Hour 1

Hour 4

Introduction

Excel 97 is much more than a mere update. This new version of the leading spreadsheet package has much greater computational ability and is considerably easier to use. The formatting functions facilitate high-quality presentation. It is even more user-friendly and is now adapted to group work.

The cell

The cell can contain 32,000 characters instead of 255 as in earlier versions.

The spreadsheet

The spreadsheet comprises 65,000 lines instead of 16,000 as in the previous version. The syntax of calculations is simplified.

Formatting

Using the WordArt drawing tools, Excel 97 is the king of formatting. Customised spreadsheet borders or highlighted titles give the spreadsheet a look which it has not had until now. AutoShapes, arrows, legends, symbols and bubbles enhance graphs.

The graphics package

The graphics package is very easy to use. In four steps the user can create excellent quality graphics. To modify a graphic object, each part may be selected with a single click. The editing of a 3D graphic object with image files and textures in the background greatly improves presentation.

73 different types of graphic object are offered.

Sharing the Excel folder

If you work as part of a network, you can at last share a folder and its spreadsheets. You have the possibility of making multi-user changes to your documents.

The Internet

From an Excel cell you can consult a site and obtain data. You can access your e-mail and the entire network. The Internet immediately recognises Internet addresses when you input them.

User friendly

The Office Assistants guide and advise you step by step. They greatly improve an interface which was perhaps a little too rigid in previous versions.

Throughout this book you will find notes which you can read or ignore. Each type of note is associated with an icon which will enable you to identify them easily:

These notes provide additional information about the subject concerned.

These notes indicate a variety of shortcuts: keyboard shortcuts, 'Wizard' options, techniques reserved for experts, etc.

These notes warn you of the risks associated with a particular action and, where necessary, show you how to avoid any pitfalls.

Hour 1

Getting to know the software

THE CONTENTS FOR THIS HOUR

- Installing Excel 97
- Starting Excel 97
- What's on the screen?
- Spreadsheets
- Cells
- Using a dialog box
- Becoming acquainted with Assistants

INSTALLING EXCEL 97

Excel 97 provides Internet access, a platform of macro commands unified with Word 97 using Visual Basic for Applications, and including surprising graphic improvements. Before using its sophisticated functions, it is recommended that you familiarise yourself with the basic screen layout and menus.

Hardware requirements

In order to install and use Excel 97 you must have:

- A PC with a 486 or Pentium processor
- Windows 95 (or a later version) or Windows NT
- At least 8 Mb of RAM (16 Mb recommended)
- A hard disk with a minimum of 10 Mb disk space available for minimum installation, 28 Mb for standard installation or 40 Mb for full installation
- A CD-ROM drive
- A Windows-compatible monitor
- A Microsoft-compatible mouse

Installing Excel 97

To install Excel 97, proceed as follows:

1. Switch on your computer and start up Windows.
2. Insert the Excel 97 CD into your CD-ROM drive.
3. Click on the Installation button.
4. Follow the instructions as they appear in the various dialog boxes of the installation program.

STARTING EXCEL 97

To start Excel 97:

1. Click on the Start button on the Taskbar.
2. Click on the Microsoft Excel option.

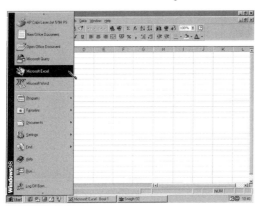

Figure 1.1: The Start button on the Taskbar and the Microsoft Excel 97 option

The Excel program is started. Sheet 1 of Book 1 appears on screen by default (Figure 1.2).

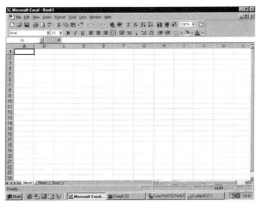

Figure 1.2: Sheet 1 of Book 1 appears by default

What's on the screen?

The Excel screen constitutes your workshop. You are going to get to know it and then customise it. Remember that you yourself will select the toolbars to be displayed and even the elements which make them up. Excel is a flexible tool if you just take the trouble to get to know it.

The Excel window

In the top right-hand corner of the screen there is an icon called Restore the window. It makes it possible to change from a full screen display to display in a window.

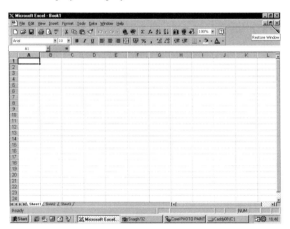

Figure 1.3: The Restore the window icon returns a window to its original size and location

If you click on it, the spreadsheet appears in a window.

The maximise icon allows you to return to full-screen display.

The icon in the form of a black cross (x) located beside the maximise and minimise icons closes the window.

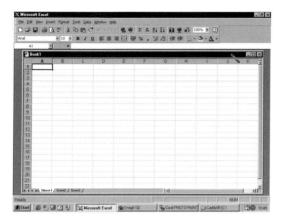

Figure 1.4: The spreadsheet appears in a window

The title bar

The title bar is located at the top of the window. It indicates the application name, i.e. "Microsoft Excel", and the name given to the workbook when this is displayed on the full screen.

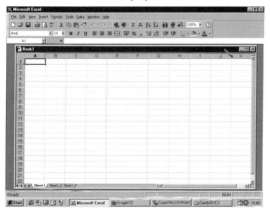

Figure 1.5: Title bar

The menu bar

The menu bar is located underneath the title bar. It indicates the names of the 9 drop-down menus.

Figure 1.6: Menu bar

The toolbar

Excel offers nine default toolbars. It allows these to be fully customised and additional bars to be created. These toolbars may be moved freely.

Figure 1.7: Standard and Formatting toolbars

Hiding a toolbar

You can hide a toolbar at any time.

Using the right-hand mouse button:

1. Click on any toolbar.
2. In the context-sensitive menu which appears, click on the toolbar which you want to show or hide.

The status bar

The status bar is located at the foot of the screen. It may be removed in order to enlarge the spreadsheet. On the left it gives information concerning the current work mode, plus the activation status of certain keyboard keys.

The formula bar

The formula bar enables you to view and modify the content of the cells of your spreadsheet. It shows the data which you are in the process of entering in the cell. When it is active, the "Cancel" and "Enter" buttons are displayed.

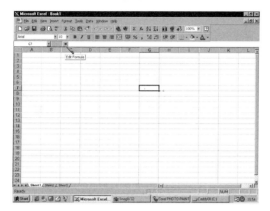

Figure 1.8: The formula bar

The Name zone

The Name zone, located below and to the left of the toolbar, gives the references of the active cell, for example "G7", if cell G7 is active.

Info-bubbles

If you position your cursor over an icon for several seconds, the function of the icon is stated simply in an info-bubble.

To deactivate info-bubbles:

1. Click on the View menu.

2. Highlight the Toolbar sub-menu.

3. Click on Customise.

4. Click on the Options tab.

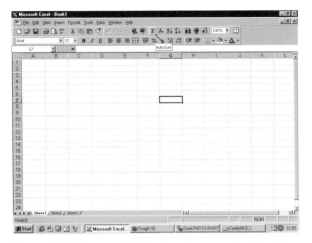

Figure 1.9: The word "AutoSum" appears in the info-bubble when you point the cursor at the icon marked Σ

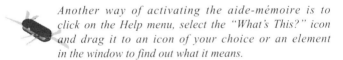

Another way of activating the aide-mémoire is to click on the Help menu, select the "What's This?" icon and drag it to an icon of your choice or an element in the window to find out what it means.

Vertical and horizontal scroll bars

The scroll bars and arrows allow you to move very quickly in order to view different sections of the spreadsheet.

You can use two methods to scroll through a spreadsheet, depending on whether you are using the mouse or the keyboard.

To scroll a column or row, click on the arrow pointing in the desired direction, located at the end of the horizontal or vertical scroll bar.

Let us imagine that you want to move to the right by one column. Columns A to G appear on your screen. In order to enter data in a cell in column H, just click on the black arrow pointing towards the right on the horizontal scroll bar.

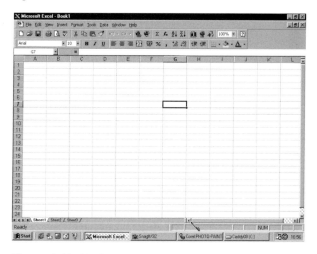

Figure 1.10: Horizontal scroll bar

SPREADSHEETS

The spreadsheet is made up of just over 4 million cells arranged in 256 columns and 16,384 rows. It is saved in a workbook. Only a small portion of this spreadsheet is shown on the screen.

A workbook comprises several spreadsheets. Excel presents three by default, but you can add others at any time.

1. Click on the Insert menu.

2. Click on the Worksheet option.

3. Validate.

You did have three worksheets displayed on screen, you now have four. To display the worksheet of your choice, click on its tab.

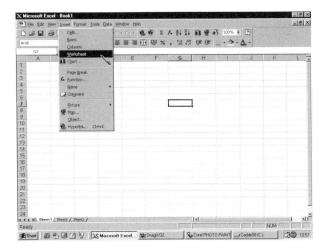

Figure 1.11: To call in another worksheet, click on the Insert menu and click on the Worksheet option

Moving around the spreadsheet using the keyboard

You can move around the spreadsheet using the keyboard. You have seven direction arrows, specific keys and the combination of these keys and arrows:

- Arrow up, to move up by one character or cell

- Arrow down, to move down by one character or cell

- Arrow left, to move left by one character or cell

- Arrow right, to move right by one character or cell

- Diagonal arrow up to left/right, called "Home", to move to the 1st cell of the current row

- Arrow up crossed by three small horizontal lines, called "Page up" (PgUp), to move up by one screen

- Arrow down crossed by three small horizontal lines, called "Page down" (PgDn), to move down by one screen

- Ctrl+PgDn: to go to the next spreadsheet

- Ctrl+PgUp: to go to the previous spreadsheet

- Ctrl+arrow right: to move to the next non-empty cell to the right or to the last cell of the row

- Ctrl+arrow left: to move to the next non-empty cell to the left or to the first cell of the row

- Ctrl+arrow down: to move to the next non-empty cell down or to the last cell of the column

- Ctrl+arrow up: to move to the next non-empty cell up or to the first cell of the column

- Ctrl+arrow Home: to move to the first cell of the worksheet

- Ctrl+End: to move to the last cell of the worksheet, the intersection of the last row and the last column which are not empty.

Cells

The cell is the basic unit of Excel. It may contain different types of data: name, text, formula, etc.

The active cell is surrounded by a thicker line. It is this one which will be affected by the next action.

Each cell is characterised by its address, which corresponds to the intersection of a row number and a column letter. Addressing may be absolute or relative. Relative addressing is the default work mode, facilitating the copying of formulae.

▰▰▰▰ Moving around the cell using the mouse

To move around a cell, just move the cursor (in the shape of a white cross) to the cell that you want to activate.

USING A DIALOG BOX

Dialog boxes are designed to give you fairly complete, even exhaustive, information on the subject in question. They are made up of several pages which are accessed by clicking on tabs. A dialog box may contain:

- **Text zones:** these are intended to be filled by a string of characters or numerical values, which you type in using the keyboard.

- **Boxes to be checked:** these contain complementary instructions for executing the command. They are activated or deactivated with a single click.

- **Option buttons:** unlike boxes to be checked, only one option can be selected to the exclusion of all others in an option zone. The active option is marked by a black circle.

- **Drop down lists;** these contain a list of pre-set replies, one of which is selected by default.

- **Buttons:** these enable you to validate or cancel your command. Some boxes will present other buttons enabling you to open several complementary dialog boxes in sequence.

- **Counters:** counters are small boxes with an arrow up and an arrow down enabling you to adjust a numerical count.

- **Close box:** the close box is an icon in the form of a cross (×). It is located in the top right-hand corner of the dialog box. If you click on it, it closes the active file.

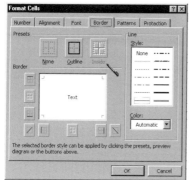

Figure 1.12: Format Cells dialog box

BECOMING ACQUAINTED WITH ASSISTANTS

Excel 97 offers nine assistants to guide you through the spreadsheet package. Office Assistant is an interactive program which dialogues with you.

Figure 1.13: Microsoft Office portrait gallery

Each of these assistants answers questions which you may ask concerning the use of specific tasks, at any time. To call them up, click on the bubble containing a question mark located at the top right corner of your screen.

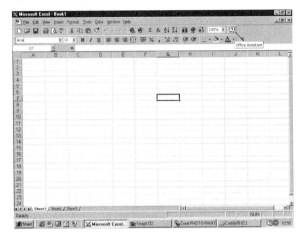

Figure 1.14: Office Assistant icon

In the dialog box which opens up, you state what you want to do. Once your question is clearly stated, you can choose between four buttons:

- Search
- Tips
- Options
- Close

If you enter the name "Office Assistant" and click on the Search button, a little character called Clippit will ask you if you want help from an Office Assistant, if you want to hide it, resize it, etc.

If you click on Options, the Presentation and Options tabs appear on screen. Options offers you a series of boxes for checking, such as React to F1, Help on assistants, Sound or even Move window if it bothers you. Selecting Presentation enables you to get to know all the Office Assistants.

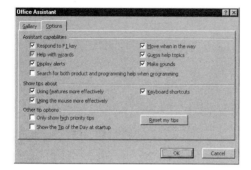

Figure 1.15: Office Assistant dialog box

The first Assistant, Clippit, gives you his tips as a well-informed and conscientious teacher. When you have a specific question to ask him, type in the key word in the text zone (e.g. "Tabulation"). Clippit then offers you a list of operations relating to tabulation. You select the one corresponding to your question.

For example, let us suppose that you wanted to insert tabs. Office Assistant offers you another increasingly specific list of operations: setting tabs, deleting or moving tabs, for example.

To set tabs, click on this command using the small white hand and you will get the answer.

So here are the nine Office Assistants which Excel offers:

- **Clippit** is your general guide.
- **The Dot** is at your side when you do not understand.
- **The Genius** takes charge of everything concerning the Office 97 environment and beyond.

- **Hoverbot** answers all your questions without necessarily understanding them.

- **Office Logo** does not have much personality, but he can be useful all the same.

- **Mother Nature** answers your obscure questions.

- **Power Pup** encourages you.

- **Scribble** is always at your heels.

- **Will** has a thus far unconfessed passion for computers.

The choice is yours!

Hour 2

Data entry

THE CONTENTS FOR THIS HOUR

- Creating a new workbook
- Renaming the active worksheet
- Opening an existing workbook
- Inputting data
- Using the financial format
- Changing the width of a column
- Undo and Redo functions
- Selecting cells

- Searching and replacing cell contents

- Clearing cell contents

- Saving a workbook

- Saving a workbook under another name

- Saving a workbook with its properties

- Changing file format

CREATING A NEW WORKBOOK

When you start up the software, a default workbook called Book 1 appears immediately. It is possible to use this workbook and rename it later.

To use a new workbook, click on the File menu and select New. In the dialog box which appears, click on Workbook, then OK.

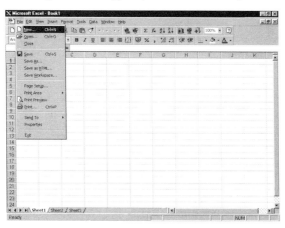

Figure 2.1: Select New in the File menu

The workbook displayed has three worksheets by default. The first of these is the active worksheet.

22

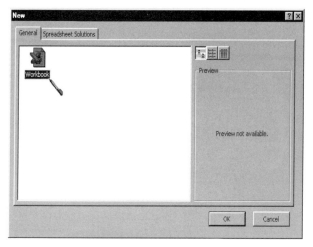

Figure 2.2: New worksheet dialog box

RENAMING THE ACTIVE WORKSHEET

We are going to rename the active worksheet Hour_02. To do this, click with the right-hand mouse button on the tab of the active worksheet at the bottom left of the screen. Click on Rename in the context menu which appears. The cursor goes to the tab to be renamed. Type in the new text, in this case Hour_02.

OPENING AN EXISTING WORKBOOK

To open an existing workbook, use the File menu, Open and then select the workbook in the dialog box which appears. You can also open one of these workbooks directly by activating the File menu, as Excel memorises the last four workbooks opened.

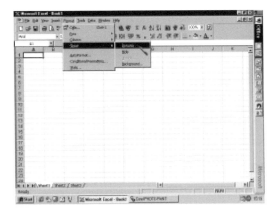

Figure 2.3: Renaming the active worksheet

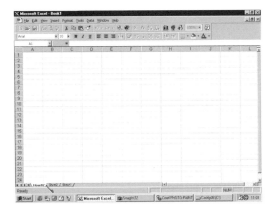

Figure 2.4: Type Hour_02 on the tab of your active worksheet

If a password has been allocated to the worksheet by the Save Options dialog box, you must enter it in order to access the document.

Figure 2.5: Password for sharing file

INPUTTING DATA

▬▬▬ Data entry in a range of cells

All you have to do is highlight a range of contiguous or non-contiguous cells in order for the cell's block of data to be moved to this range during data entry.

The data contained in the active cell, during or after entry, are displayed in the formula bar. To amend data, click on the text displayed in this bar or use key F2.

▬▬▬ Entering numbers

To enter a number, type in the first digit preceded by a + or –, if necessary. The other characters accepted are (,) , / , * , E and F.

▬▬▬ Entering dates and times

The software memorises dates and times in the form of numeric series. Excel uses the calendar from 1900: serial numbers correspond to dates between 1 January 1900 and 31 December 9999.

▬▬▬ To change the date system:

1. Click on the Tools menu
2. Select Options
3. Click on the Calculation tab
4. Check or uncheck the 1904 date system box

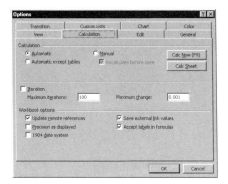

Figure 2.6: To change the date system, check or uncheck the 1904 date system box

Entering text

Excel considers as text everything which is not a name, date, time or formula. A text may be composed of figures, letters or symbols, but may not exceed 32,000 characters per cell.

In order to detail the steps to follow in entering text, let us take an example. Let us say that you want to evaluate how much it will cost you to prepare a regional dish from Alsace, the Baeckhoffe (a stew containing 3 meats).

In column A, you enter the name of the ingredients, in column B, the quantities necessary, and in column C, the price of these ingredients.

1. Start by clicking on cell C1.

2. Type the words Ingredients, Weight and Price in cells A1, B1 and C1 respectively. When you enter your text, it appears simultaneously in the formula bar. If you make a mistake, use the Backspace key.

3. When you have typed Price, confirm what you have entered by pressing Enter.

4. Click on the next cell.

5. Once the column headers are inserted, enter the following recipe in the columns, in accordance with the specimen.

 Recipe for Baeckhoffe, or Alsace stew, found on the Internet.
Marinade 500 g of brisket of beef in Alsace wine for 24 hours, together with 500 g of shoulder of lamb and 500 g of shoulder of pork cut into pieces.
In an earthenware pot, lay your meat on a layer of sliced potatoes. Cover it with a layer of sliced onions, a layer of potatoes and a final layer of onions. Cover with Alsace wine and cook in the oven for around 2½ hours, then serve. You can accompany this dish with a bottle of "Pinot" from Alsace.

When you type the text of column A, it overflows into column B, and when you enter the contents of column B, the text of column A which overflowed appears to be covered. You must then adapt the width of the columns and improve the presentation as a whole.

USING THE FINANCIAL FORMAT

Any prices to be entered in a chart may be displayed in the form of whole numbers, in pounds, and with thousand separators in the case of large figures.

In order to have access to these various presentations:

1. Click on the Format menu

2. Select Cells

3. Click on the Cell format tab

4. Select Currency

Currency formats are used for general monetary values. Use the accounting formats to align decimals in a column.

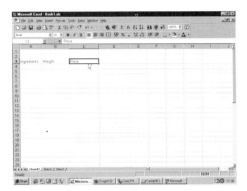

Figure 2.7: Entering data in columns A, B and C

The currency icon applies the International Currency style to the cells highlighted. Depending on the country selected in the Windows Regional Settings dialog box, it is possible for the International Currency Style button to be displayed instead of the Currency Style button.

CHANGING THE WIDTH OF A COLUMN

The simplest way of adapting the width of column A is to position the mouse pointer on the line between columns A and B. The pointer turns into a two-way arrow. Click and move the mouse to the desired width.

The standard column width corresponds to the average number of digits between 0 and 9 which may be contained in a cell according to the font selected. To adjust the width of the column in keeping with its content, double-click on the border to the right of the column header.

Defining a default column width has the effect of adjusting all columns to the same width, except for those previously modified.

UNDO AND REDO FUNCTIONS

▬▬▬ Using the keyboard

Mistakes are not final. By holding down the Ctrl key at the same time as pressing Z (Ctrl+Z), you can undo your last action. If you again press on these keys, you undo the action before last, and so on for sixteen levels. To repeat a keystroke, just press Ctrl+Y.

▬▬▬ Using the mouse

To undo an action using the mouse, click on the icon in the form of a blue arrow pointing to the left on the Standard toolbar. The black arrow located to its right gives you access to a drop-down list of the latest actions which may be undone.

The Redo icon (blue arrow pointing to the right) cancels the Undo command. The black arrow also gives you access to a drop-down list of the most recent actions which may be cancelled.

SELECTING CELLS

Selecting cells is a basic operation using the spreadsheet package. It consists in highlighting several cells so as to apply a command to them.

You can highlight a group of cells, whether contiguous or not.

- **Contiguous cells:** click and drag from the first cell in the zone.

- **Range of cells:** click on the first cell, then on the last, while holding the Caps key down.

- **Non-contiguous cells:** click while holding the Ctrl key down.

- **Row or column:** click on the row number or column letter.

- **Entire chart:** click underneath the active cell's reference at the top left-hand corner of the chart.

There are many keyboard shortcuts for selecting entire zones:

1. Click on the Edit menu

2. Select Go To

3. Click on the Cells button

4. Check the boxes in the Select cells dialog box

Figure 2.8: Select cells dialog box

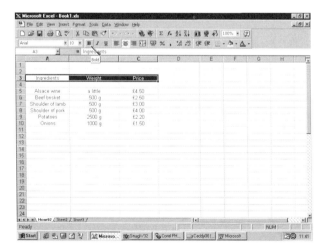

Figure 2.9: Select the Bold icon to put your characters in bold typeface

Once your chart is complete, you will perhaps want to put the column headers into bold. To do this, highlight the three cells concerned. Go to the first, cell A3. Click and drag as far as cell C3. Then release the mouse button. All three cells are highlighted. The first remains black on white and the others are reversed, i.e. white on a black background. Now just click on the tool representing bold.

SEARCHING AND REPLACING CELL CONTENTS

To search and replace the contents of a cell:

1. Select the range of cells that you want to replace

2. Click on the Edit menu, then click on Replace

3. In the Search box, enter the text or numbers that you want to replace

4. In the Replace by box, type the replacement characters

5. Click on Next

6. To replace data one at a time, click each time on Replace

7. If you want to replace all terms at once, click on Replace all

8. To cancel a search, press Cancel

CLEARING CELL CONTENTS

1. Select the cells, row or columns that you want to clear

2. Click on the Edit menu, then click on Clear. A sub-menu appears on the screen allowing you to choose between several options:

   • All

   • Formats

   • Content

   • Notes

SAVING A WORKBOOK

When your work is sufficiently advanced, you should save it on the hard disk. In this way you do not risk losing it.

Windows 95 uses the word Document to designate data saved on disks, while Word, Excel and Access still retain the term File in menus.

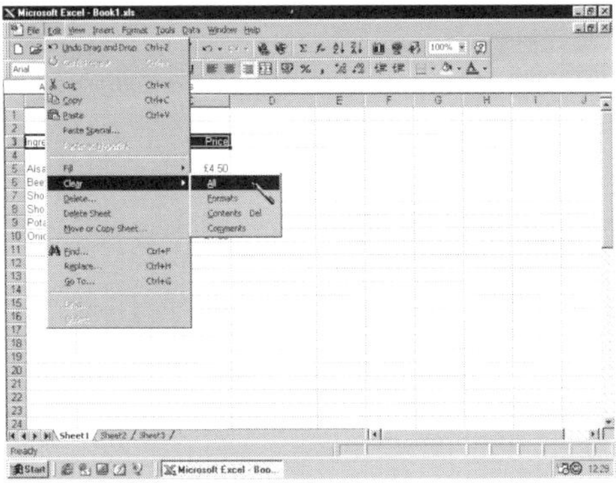

Figure 2.10: Select the options Delete and All to delete the entire contents of a cell

To save:

1. Click on the File menu
2. Click on Save or the diskette icon on the toolbar
3. If the file does not already have a name, the default name Workbook1 is suggested. Change to the name of your choice, in this case Quick_course
4. Choose a directory and click on the Save button.

In order to see the list of workbooks in the memory, click on the Window menu.

▰▰▰ Information on a workbook

The General tab gives various information on the file selected. Click on the File menu, select Properties, then click on the General tab.

SAVING A WORKBOOK UNDER ANOTHER NAME

You can change the name of your workbook and save it on another disk.

1. Click on the File menu
2. Select Save as. In the dialog box which appears, select the drive on which you want to save your workbook.
3. In the File name text box, enter the new name that you are going to give to your workbook

Once the workbook is named and saved, just click on the Save icon to save changes.

Figure 2.11 illustrates this operation, assuming that you choose drive D, the directory Course, and Excel 97 as the new name for your workbook.

SAVING A WORKBOOK WITH ITS PROPERTIES

To save a workbook with its properties:

1. Click on the File menu
2. Select Properties
3. Click on the Summary tab
4. Complete the text boxes relating to the title, subject, etc.
5. Add a comment, if necessary
6. Validate by clicking on OK

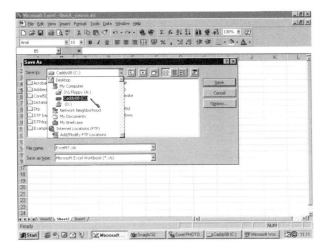

Figure 2.11: Select the destination directory and the new name of your workbook

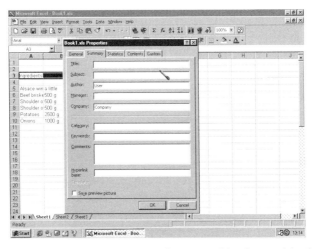

Figure 2.12: The properties of your workbook saved in the Summary tab of the Properties dialog box

 34

You can parameterise the saving of the sheet so that a backup copy is made when you save it. This operation allows you to retain the previous version with the suffix BAK. Click on the File menu, click on Save as, then click on the Options button and check the option Create Backup Copy.

Changing file format

To facilitate running the spreadsheet with other software or computers (e.g. Mac), it is possible to select the save format.

1. Click on the File menu

2. Select Save as

3. In the list Save as type, select the file format which you want.

The main types of file

The main types of file are as follows:

- Microsoft Excel Workbook (extension XLS)

- Template   Excel type worksheet (extension XLT)

- Excel 5   Worksheet of former Excel versions

- SYLK   To Multiplan or pre-Excel 1.5

- Text   To word-processor, space separators or tabulation

- CSV   To word-processor

- WKS WKI   To Lotus

- Mac   To Mac

Hour 3

Formatting a chart

THE CONTENTS FOR THIS HOUR

- Drag-and-Drop function
- Entering a chart title
- Aligning a title
- Merging cells and centring
- Changing character size and font
- Changing the height of a row
- Changing the width of a column
- Orientation of text
- Fitting text

- Adding a border

- Adding patterns

- Shading a cell

- AutoFormat

DRAG-AND-DROP FUNCTION

Before discovering the tools which you have in Excel for formatting your chart, it is important to know how to move one or more cells using the Drag-and-Drop function.

1. Highlight zone C10:A1, i.e. the zone encompassing the whole of your chart.

2. Place your cursor on the border of the zone selected. It turns into a white arrow.

3. Click and hold the mouse button down.

4. Drag the pointer to a new location, namely zone B6:D15. While being moved, the border of the selected area is dark grey.

5. Release the mouse button. If you release it too soon, your selected zone may be moved to the wrong place. Just click on the Undo icon on the toolbar or press Crtl+2 to undo the operation.

ENTERING A CHART TITLE

To format the title of your chart you must obviously enter it first:

1. Place the cursor at the intersection of line 1 and column B, i.e. in cell B1.

2. Click. The selection marker surrounds the cell.

3. Enter the title Baeckhoffe.

4. Validate by pressing the Enter key.

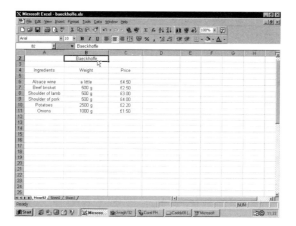

Figure 3.1: Before formatting your chart, enter its title. In this illustration, the alignment has been changed from the default left alignment to being centred.

ALIGNING A TITLE

You will then see that your title is aligned with the left side of cell B1. Excel 97 aligns text with the left side of the cell by default. Times, dates and numbers are aligned with the right side. You can change this alignment and choose between the options of the formatting toolbar:

- **Left alignment:** aligns selected text, numbers or integrated objects to the left, without right justification

- **Right alignment:** aligns selected text, numbers or integrated objects to the right, without left justification.

- **Centre:** centres selected text, numbers or integrated objects (Figure 3.1).

Select your title. Click on the Centre icon on the formatting toolbar. You can repeat the same operation for the other chart data, e.g. for chart subtitles.

MERGING CELLS AND CENTRING

The Merge and centre icon combines 2 adjacent cells or more which
have been selected, to create a single cell. The resulting merged cell
contains only the data located in the top left corner of the selection,
which are centred inside the new cell.

To centre a title over several columns, you must start by selecting
the columns over which your title is to be centred. Let us suppose
that you want to centre your title "Baeckhoffe" over all of the
columns of your chart. To do this, select zone B6:D6 and click on
the Merge and centre icon.

Your title is centred over columns B, C and D.

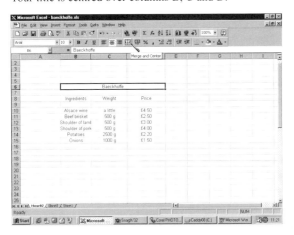

Figure 3.2: Merge the cells of a chart title

CHANGING CHARACTER SIZE AND FONT

With Windows 95 you have True Type character fonts. The
advantage of this is that the same font will be used on the printer
and on the screen and all of them can be printed on any printer.

The True Type designation is a double T beside each font. The default font, Times New Roman, provides a standard presentation. It applies to new documents created using the active template.

Changing character font

Let us suppose that you do not like the character font.

1. Select your chart, i.e. zone B6:D15.

2. Click on the Format menu.

3. Click on the Cell option.

4. Select the Font tab.

5. Click on Bodoni Bk BT.

The character font of your chart is now Bodoni Bk BT, 11 point size.

Changing size

If the characters of your chart are too large, select a smaller size.

1. Select the whole of your chart area, i.e. zone B6:D15.

2. Then Click on the Format menu.

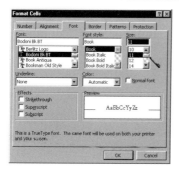

Figure 3.3: Changing character font and size

3. Select the Cell option

4. Then click on the Font tab

5. Click on point size 11 of the font Bodoni Bk BT, the one used for the chart.

CHANGING THE HEIGHT OF A ROW

You can use two different techniques to change the height of a row.

Using the interface

The ends of the horizontal lines separating the cells may be moved. After selecting the cell zone, the height of which you wish to change, position your cursor at the end of a horizontal line. It turns into a double vertical black arrow. Let us suppose that the cells receiving the subtitles of your chart are not high enough.

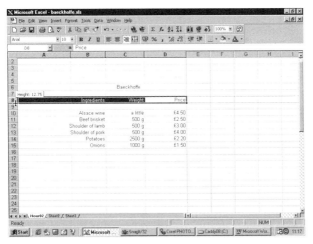

Figure 3.4: Changing the height of a chart row using the interface

1. Select zone A8:D8
2. Place your cursor at the top of the row
3. Adjust the row height to suit your requirements. Let us suppose that it is not the standard height 12, but height 17.25 that you want.
4. Keep the left mouse button pressed down, once range 8 is selected.
5. Drag the cursor "Double vertical arrow" downwards to the size you want, to increase the height of the row.

Using the Format menu

1. Select the subtitles zone B8:D8
2. Click on the Format menu
3. Select the Row sub-menu
4. Click on height
5. In the dialog box, enter the desired row height: 17.25

Figure 3.5: Modifying the height of a chart row using the Format menu

CHANGING THE WIDTH OF A COLUMN

You can use two different techniques to change the width of a column.

Using the interface

The lines separating column headers can be moved at will. Click on the line separating the headers of columns B and C. Your cursor then turns into a two-way arrow. Drag it towards the right until you obtain the value you want, 17.71 for example.

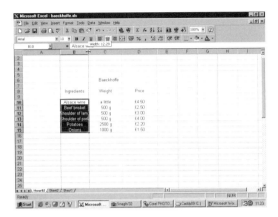

Figure 3.6: Modifying the width of a column using the interface

Using the Format menu

ORIENTATION OF TEXT

The text inside a cell may be re-orientated by up to 90°. In this way you can slant your text up or down.

1. Select the subtitles of your chart

2. Click on the Format menu

3. Call in the Cell sub-menu

4. Click on the Alignment tab

5. Select the Orientation option

6. Select value 7 on the counter.

Your subtitles slant upwards by 7°, which may have a positive feel but is not necessarily very good on an aesthetic level! You can choose the orientation which best suits the message that you want to give.

44

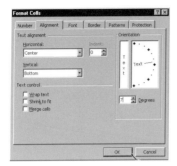

Figure 3.7: Slanting your subtitles upwards by 7 degrees

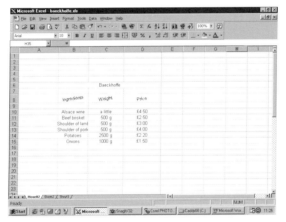

Figure 3.8: Graphics with a positive feel!

If you have saved a workbook in another file format, it is possible for the text rotation format to be lost. Most file formats do not include the full 180° rotation (from +90° to –90°) which Microsoft Excel 97 allows. Previous versions of Microsoft Excel allowed text rotation of +90°, 0° or –90°. If the angle of rotation specified cannot be supported in another file format, the text is not pivoted.

Fitting text

Let us suppose this time that your subtitles are much wider than the cell.

1. Click on the Format menu
2. Click on the Cell sub-menu
3. Click on the Alignment option
4. Check the Fit box

Your title fits the available width of the cell.

Adding a border

Using the interface

To add a border using the interface:

1. Highlight your chart.

Figure 3.9: Add a border using the Border icon

2. Click on the Border menu
3. Click on the icon in the form of an outline

Your table is framed.

Using the menu

You can modify the thickness and appearance of your border at any time if the border which you have selected does not seem thick enough or seems unsuitable.

1. Highlight your chart

2. Click on the Format menu

3. Select the Cell sub-menu

4. Click on the Border tab

5. Click on the Outline option and the line style which you want

6. Validate with OK

The border of your chart is customised.

Figure 3.10: Add a border to your chart using the menu

Modifying the colour of a line or the border around an object drawn

1. Select the object which you wish to modify

2. On the Drawing toolbar, click on the arrow opposite Line colour

3. Click on the desired colour.

If the desired colour is not displayed:

1. Click on Other colours

2. Click on a colour under the Standard tab

3. Click on the Customise tab to create a customised colour

4. Validate by clicking on OK.

If you want to print the same border on cells separated by a page break, while the border only appears on one page, use the Cell command on the Format menu to apply an inner border. For example, to print a border at the foot of the last row of a page and to use this border at the top of the first row of the next page, select the rows either side of the page break, then click on Cell in the Format menu. Click on the Border tab, then on the Inner button under Pre-selections. Under Border, delete the vertical border by clicking on it in the summary diagram.

ADDING PATTERNS

With the aim of always doing better, you can enhance your cells with patterns:

1. Highlight the range of cells B6:D6 which contains your title, "Baeckhoffe".

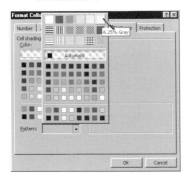

Figure 3.11: Selecting a pattern

2. Click on the Format menu

3. Select the Cell sub-menu

4. Click on the Pattern tab

5. Click on the Patterns list

6. Select a white with black dots background pattern giving the effect of grey for a value of 6.25%

Your chart is improving by the minute!

Adding background patterns to the whole worksheet

To add a background pattern to the whole worksheet:

1. Click on the worksheet to which you want to add a background pattern

2. Click on the Format menu

3. Point to Worksheet

4. Click on Background

5. Then select the graphics file to use for the background pattern

The graphic selected is reproduced throughout the worksheet. You can apply plain coloured shading to cells containing data.

If the Background command is not available, check whether you have selected only a single worksheet.

SHADING A CELL

To make the subtitles row stand out, you can, for example, shade the cells.

1. Highlight your zone B8:D8

2. Click on the Format menu

3. Click on the Cell sub-menu

4. Click on the Patterns tab

5. Click on a colour under the Cell Shading option

AUTOFORMAT

To format an entire list or large range comprising different elements, such as column and row labels, summary totals and detailed data, you can apply to them a pre-set chart template called "autoformat". This template uses different formats depending on the nature of the chart elements.

To apply several formats at once and ensure the consistency of cell formatting, you can apply a style to these.

If you feel that the appearance of your presentation could be further improved, use the autoformat feature.

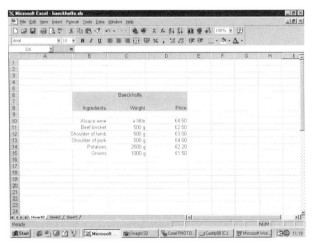

Figure 3.12: Your chart is now automatically formatted, giving it a professional look!

1. Highlight your chart

2. Click on the Format menu

3. Click on the AutoFormat option. A choice of 17 automatic formats for your chart is offered

4. Choose List 2

Copying the formatting of a range of cells to another range

To copy the formatting of a range of cells to another range, you can use the Copy format icon on the Standard toolbar. This icon enables you to copy the format of the object selected, then to apply it to the object or text on which you click.

To copy the format of several elements, double click on the Copy format icon, then click on each element to be formatted. Once the operation is complete, press Escape or click again.

Hour 4

WordArt

THE CONTENTS FOR THIS HOUR

- Drawing graphical objects
- Copying graphics
- Importing graphics
- Inserting a WORDART object
- Using clip art
- Adjusting the lighting of a 3D object
- Modifying a 3D effect
- Adding a shadow

WordArt makes it possible to enliven documents by presenting them attractively according to personal taste. This hour is devoted to the production of graphics by using standard tools which nevertheless allow the user flexibility.

DRAWING GRAPHICAL OBJECTS

The AutoShapes menu of the Drawing toolbar contains several categories of predefined drawing objects. In total you have a choice of 100 automatic shapes.

Click on a shape then drag the mouse cursor in order to achieve the size you want it to be.

You can not only turn, tilt and colour shapes, but also combine them with other standard shapes and drawing objects such as lines and rectangles.

Many shapes have a selection handle which you can use to change an option, such as the size and ends of an arrow.

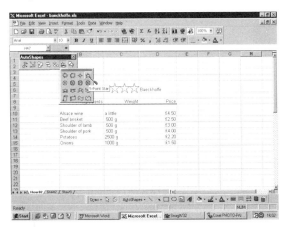

Figure 4.1: Inserting automatic shapes to enhance your chart

At any time you can decide to colour the inside of your automatic shape or its outline.

Colouring (filling) an automatic shape

To colour (fill) your automatic shape:

1. Select your automatic shape.
2. Select the Fill icon of the Drawing toolbar.
3. Click on the colour of your choice.
4. Confirm by pressing Enter.

Colouring the outline of an automatic shape

To change the outline colour of your automatic shape:

1. Select your automatic shape.
2. Select the Line colour icon from the Drawing toolbar.
3. Click on the colour of your choice.
4. Confirm by pressing Enter.

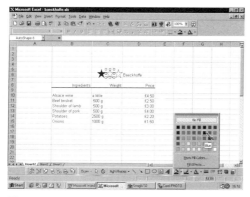

Figure 4.2: Colouring your automatic shape and its outline

▬▬▬ Writing inside an automatic shape

Once your automatic shape has been inserted, you can write inside it.

1. For example, select the Heart shape. Your cursor becomes a small cross.

2. Place this small cross at the point on the chart where you want it, keeping the left-hand mouse button pressed down.

3. Click on the Text Box icon in order to be able to insert text inside the automatic shape.

Your cursor becomes a yellow cross which you move inside the automatic Heart shape. You then simply have to write the text of your choice inside.

COPYING GRAPHICS

You can copy a group of spreadsheet cells or a graph and paste it in another workbook or application in the form of an image.

1. Select the cells or graph.

2. Keep the Caps button pressed down.

3. Click on the Edit menu.

4. Click on Copy image.

5. Select the spreadsheet or document into which you want to paste the object.

6. Use the application's paste command.

IMPORTING GRAPHICS

If you have created a graphic object in another application, you can copy it and paste it into a graph or spreadsheet.

To import an entire graphics file, click on Image in the Insert menu, then click on From file.

You can install numerous graphic filters.

If you have installed Microsoft Clip Gallery using Microsoft Office, you can insert sounds and films as well as images from the library.

If you have installed Microsoft Photo Editor, you can scan and import photographs.

INSERTING A WORDART OBJECT

In previous versions of Microsoft Office, text effects were created using the WordArt program which came with Office. In Office 97, you can create these effects directly in your application using Insert WordArt object, a new tool on the Drawing toolbar which also has new functions, such as 3D effects and Filling textures.

With WordArt you can add 3D effects to lines, automatic shapes and freeform drawn objects using the 3D effects icon on the Drawing toolbar. The 3D options enable you to modify the depth of a drawing and its colour, angle, direction of lighting and surface reflection.

1. Open your spreadsheet.
2. Install your WordArt toolbar.
3. Select your title "Baeckhoffe".
4. Delete it by pressing the Del key.
5. Position your cursor where you want to insert your new title with special WordArt effects.
6. Click on the Insert WordArt object icon.
7. Select the WordArt effect that you want.
8. Enter your text in the dialog box, adjusting the font size.
9. Confirm by pressing Enter.

Your title appears in your chart in 3D.

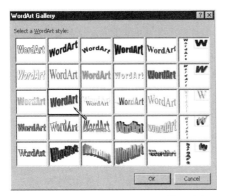

Figure 4.3: Enhancing your title with a predefined WordArt effect

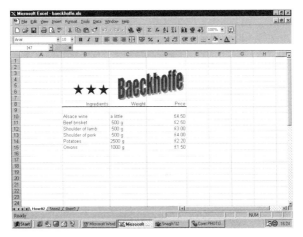

Figure 4.4: A 3D title appears in your chart

Free rotation

You can rotate your title freely.

1. Select your title.

2. Click on the Free rotation icon. The cursor then turns into a circular black arrow indicating a rotational movement.

3. Give your title the angle of rotation you require.

4. Activate the small black rotating arrow handle to give your title the desired angle.

Figure 4.5: The Free rotation icon and the handle enabling you to pivot the WordArt object

If the WordArt program is already installed on your computer, it is retained when Office 97 is installed, but it is likely that you will want to use the new tool Insert WordArt object in order to create your text effects. Text effects created in the WordArt program are not automatically converted into new animated objects.

Predefined rotation

In addition to the Free rotation icon, there are four predefined rotation icons:

- **Rotate left:** turns the selected objected through 90° to the left.

- **Rotate right:** turns the selected object through 90° to the right.

- **Flip Horizontal:** flips the selected objected horizontally through 180°.

- **Flip Vertical:** flips the selected object vertically through 180°.

These commands are not available if the object selected cannot be turned, i.e. in the case of an OLE object or image.

ABC icon

The WordArt Shape option represented by the ABC icon enables you to give to your title and its new orientation one of the 40 available looks, such as:

- stop sign
- upward triangle
- upward chevron
- downward arc
- semicircle
- compressed
- narrow
- fat

Choose the Inflate bottom option, for example.

Your title now has the predefined 3D WordArt effect and the Inflate bottom effect.

You cannot display the WordArt object in Flat mode or spellcheck it.

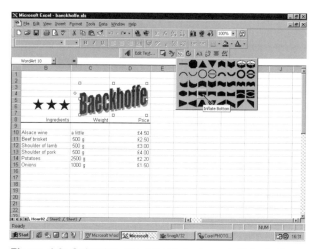

Figure 4.6: Selecting the WordArt shape Inflate bottom

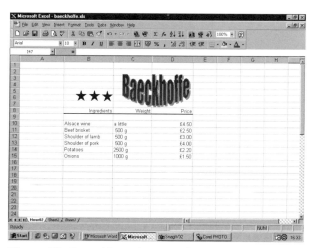

Figure 4.7: Your title and its new format

The Same height icon

The Same height icon allocates the same height to all the letters of the WordArt object selected.

Vertical text icon

The Vertical text icon writes the letters of the WordArt object selected vertically.

USING CLIPART

What is Clipart?

Clipart is a computerised drawing supplied in a library of images to serve as illustrations. Clipart, or clips, are often very rudimentary. They usually help out when the user has no illustration for his or her texts and charts. The drawback is that these small drawings are available to everybody. Employ these ready-to-use graphics with moderation!

Inserting Clipart from other applications

Microsoft Office offers you a wide choice of graphics. You can use them, for example, as a personal logo to illustrate your invoices, charts and documents. It is very simple to find them.

1. Click on Insert.

2. Select the Picture option.

3. Click on the Clipart images submenu.

4. Make an initial thematic selection: 'Plants' rather than 'Buildings'.

5. Then select the rose.

6. Click on the Insert command button.

The Clipart representing a rose is inserted where you have indicated.

ADJUSTING THE LIGHTING OF A 3D OBJECT

You are now going to create another 3D title.

1. Select your title.

2. Click on the Predefined Effects WordArt icon which presents the Word palette as a backdrop. This icon enables you to modify the form of your title without having to rewrite it.

3. Click on the predefined effect you want.

4. Confirm by selecting OK. Your new title appears in 3D on your chart.

5. Select this new WordArt object, i.e. your title in 3D.

6. Click on the 3D effects icon on the toolbar and then on the lighting icon.

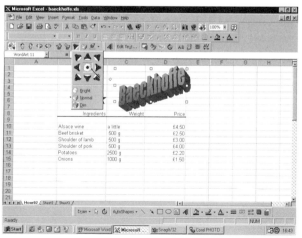

Figure 4.8: Selecting a lighting option

You can adjust the intensity and direction of lighting at the same time.

1. Start by adjusting the intensity. There are three options:

- Bright

- Normal

- Dim

2. Click on Bright.

3. Adjust the direction of lighting. You can choose between several possibilities:

- left profile

- right profile

- from above

- from below

- central

4. Select central lighting, for example.

The lighting of your title is immediately changed.

MODIFYING A 3D EFFECT

To change the 3D effect of the title of your chart, click on 3D effects on the Drawing toolbar, then use the tools of the 3D effects toolbar.

The ten icons of the 3D effects toolbar give you details concerning:

- 3D/2D display: applies 3D format to the selected object using the default 3D settings, or cancels the 3D effect. 3D effects and shadowing are mutually exclusive. If you activate 3D effects, shadow settings are deactivated, and vice versa.

- Tilt Down: the Tilt Down icon tilts the 3D effect downwards by 6° about a horizontal axis. To make it tilt as far as the next point, at 45°, hold down the Caps key and click on the Tilt Down icon.

- Tilt Up: the Tilt Up icon tilts the 3D effect upwards by 6° about a horizontal axis. To tilt it as far as the next point, at 45°, hold the Caps key down and click on the Tilt Up icon.

- Tilt Right: the Tilt Right icon tilts the 3D effect to the right by 6° about a vertical axis. To tilt it as far as the next point, at 45°, hold the Caps key down and click on the Tilt Right icon.

- Tilt Left: the Tilt Left icon tilts the 3D effect to the left by 6° about a vertical axis. To tilt it as far as the next point, at 45°, hold the Caps key down and click on the Tilt Left icon.

- Depth: adjusts the depth of a 3D shape from 0 points to infinity. A customised option enables you to define the number of points yourself.

- Direction: adjusts the perspective that you want to give to your volume.

- Lighting: adjusts the lighting of your volume using nine different angles.

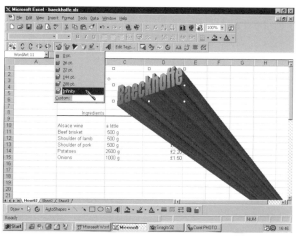

Figure 4.9: Your title with an 'Infinity' depth effect

- Surface: adjusts the appearance that you want to give to your volume. There are four options: wire frame, matte, plastic and metal.

- 3D colour (automatic): defines the colour that you want to give to your volume. This may be standard or customised.

Select your title 'Baeckhoffe'. Click on the Depth icon under 3D effects. Set the depth that you want to give to your title, in points: 72 points, 144 points, or infinity, for example.

ADDING A SHADOW

You can add a shadow to a shape or drawing by clicking on the Shadow icon on the Drawing toolbar. Twenty options are offered, including:

- **Nudge Shadow Up:** nudges the shadow given to selected objects upwards in increments.

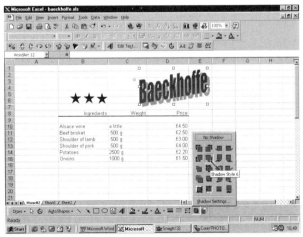

Figure 4.10: Your title enhanced by a shadow of amplitude 6

- **Nudge Shadow Down:** nudges the shadow given to selected objects downwards in increments.

- **Nudge Shadow Left:** nudges the shadow given to selected objects to the left in increments.

- **Nudge Shadow Right:** nudges the shadow given to selected objects to the right in increments.

1. Choose, for example, Shadow style 6.

2. Confirm by pressing enter. Your title and its shadow effect appear on your chart.

 The Shadow On/Off icon activates the shadow effects given to the selected object using default settings, or deactivates them. Shadow effects and 3D effects are mutually exclusive. If you activate Shadow effects, all 3D effects will be deactivated automatically, and vice versa.

Hour 5

Carrying out
simple operations

THE CONTENTS FOR THIS HOUR

- Addition
- Subtraction
- Multiplication
- Division
- Constructing a formula

- Copying a formula
- Calculating an average
- Calculating an average using the Function Wizard
- Using matrix formulae

With Microsoft Excel you can create a wide variety of formulae, whether you need to carry out simple or more complex operations.

You will use predefined formulae for simple calculations.

To carry out several calculations simultaneously to yield one or more results, you may use a matrix formula.

If you want to display the total value of a range of cells, use the automatic calculation function.

When you select cells, Microsoft Excel displays the total of this range in the status bar.

ADDITION

The following operations are carried out from the Grafico chart.

When your spreadsheet contains several subtotals generated by the Sum function, you can find the aggregate total using the AutoSum function. To determine an aggregate total, click on a cell located below and to the right of the range containing the subtotals, then click on the AutoSum button.

To calculate the total articles sold by Grafico, proceed as follows:

1. Click on cell B14 which is to receive the total.
2. Type =. This sign indicates to Excel that a formula is being created.
3. Select all the cells that you want to include in this formula as described in 4-6 below.

4. Click on cell B9 containing the value 75. It is the first value in your addition. Your cell is highlighted by flashing dots. B9 also appears in the formula bar.

5. Then type +. This addition sign is called an 'operator'.

6. Once you have entered the operator, click on the next cell, i.e. B10, then add +. Repeat this operation as far as cell B12.

7. Confirm by pressing Enter. Your total appears in cell B14.

Do not forget to enter = before entering the formula. Otherwise, Excel does not understand that you are going into operational mode.

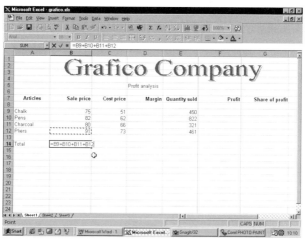

Figure 5.1: Carrying out addition using Excel 97

Figure 5.2: The total appears in the cell containing the formula

AutoSum

Another method available is to use the AutoSum button on the standard toolbar. To do this, proceed as follows:

1. Click in cell B14, which is to receive the total.

2. Click on the AutoSum button. The range of cells being added together appears in the formula bar and in the totals cell.

3. Confirm by pressing Enter. Your total appears in cell B14.

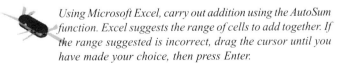

Using Microsoft Excel, carry out addition using the AutoSum function. Excel suggests the range of cells to add together. If the range suggested is incorrect, drag the cursor until you have made your choice, then press Enter.

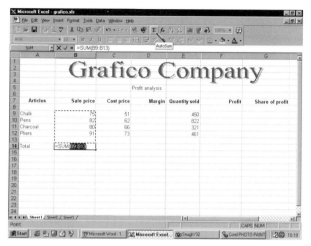

Figure 5.3: Carrying out addition using the AutoSum button

Subtotals

If your spreadsheet contains several subtotals generated using the Sum function, you can determine the aggregate total of these values using the AutoSum function. To arrive at an aggregate total, click on a cell located below or to the right of the range containing the subtotals, then click on the AutoSum button.

The different calculation operators in formulae

Operators indicate the type of calculation which you wish to carry out on the elements of a formula.

Microsoft Excel offers four different types of calculation operator:

- Arithmetical operators: these carry out basic mathematical operations, such as addition, subtraction or multiplication, combine numbers and produce numerical results.

- Logical operators: these compare two values then produce the logical value TRUE or FALSE.

- Text operator: this combines one or more text values to give a single text element.

- Reference zone operators: these combine ranges of cells in order to carry out calculations.

The following tables show the operators of each of these categories.

Arithmetical operators

+	Addition
-	Subtraction
*	Multiplication
/	Division
%	Percent
^	The exponent (to the power of)

Logical operators

=	Equal to
>	Greater than
<	Less than
>=	Greater than or equal to
<=	Less than or equal to
<>	Not equal to

Text operator

&	Links two values to give a continuous text value.

Reference zone operators

:	Range operator which allocates a reference to all the cells between two references, including the two references
,	Operator which combines several references in a single reference.

SUBTRACTION

Let us assume that you want to enter in cell B16 the result of subtracting cell B14 from B15. To do this, proceed as follows.

1. Click in the cell which is to receive the result of the subtraction (cell B16 in our example).

2. Enter the = sign then select cell B14. Enter the - sign and then click in cell B15.

3. Confirm by pressing Enter. The result of your subtraction is shown in cell B16.

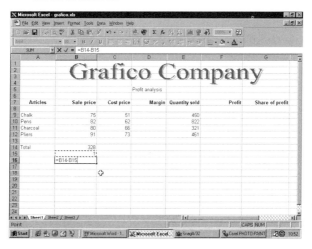

Figure 5.4: Carrying out subtraction

MULTIPLICATION

This time you are going to multiply cell B14 with cell B15, and enter the result of this operation in cell B16. Proceed as follows.

1. Click in the cell which is to receive the result of the multiplication (cell B16 in our example).

2. Enter the = sign indicating to Excel 97 that you are going into operational mode.

3. Then click on the value in cell B14.

4. Enter the multiplication sign (*) in cell B16.

5. Click on cell B15.

6. Confirm by pressing Enter. The result of the multiplication appears in cell B16.

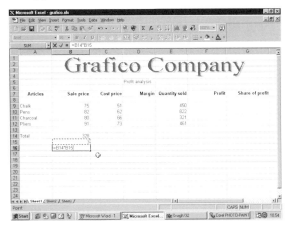

Figure 5.5: Carrying out multiplication

DIVISION

Let us assume that you want to enter in cell B16 the result of dividing cell B14 by cell B15. To do this, proceed as follows.

1. Click in cell B16 which is to receive the result of the division.

2. Enter the =sign in this cell, indicating to Excel 97 that you are going into operational mode.

3. Click in cell B14, then enter the division operator (/) in cell B16.

 76

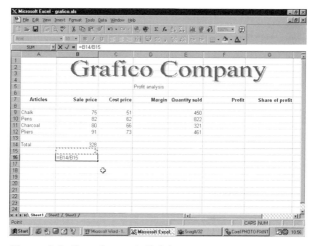

Figure 5.6: Carrying out division

4. Click in cell B15 and confirm by pressing the Enter key. The result of the division is shown in cell B16.

Constructing a formula

Formulae calculate the values in a certain syntactical order. All Microsoft Excel formulae begin with the sign = followed by the calculation.

In the chart of the Grafico company, the column 'Margin' is the result of a calculation using the columns 'Sale price' and 'Cost price'.

Margin = sale price - cost price

You are going to create a formula for the first article, chalk. You will copy it for the other articles. The details are as follows: the sale price of the chalk is in cell B9, the cost price is in cell C9 and we want to put the result in cell D9. Proceed as follows.

1. Click on D9, the cell which is to receive the margin on chalk, then type = to indicate to Excel 97 that this is a calculation formula.

2. Click on cell B9, the sale price of the chalk. It appears surrounded by flashing dots and the formula bar shows =B9.

3. Then type the - sign (subtraction operator). The dots disappear. Excel 97 is waiting for the address of the cell to subtract.

4. Click on C9, the cost price of the chalk. Confirm by pressing Enter. The number 24 appears, the value of the margin achieved; the formula bar displays the formula.

Figure 5.7: Calculate a margin using Excel 97

COPYING A FORMULA

When you move a formula, the cell references included in the formula are not modified. When you copy a formula, the absolute cell references are not modified, unlike the relative cell references.

To calculate the margin achieved on sales of other articles, just copy the formula from cell D9. You can choose the method which suits you best from among the three methods described below.

First method:

1. Select the range D9:D12.

2. Click on the Edit menu.

3. Select the options Copy and Below.

The margins are shown for all the articles.

Second method:

1. Click on cell D9 and move the mouse cursor to the copy handle shaped like a little black cross, to the bottom right-hand corner of the cell.

2. Keep the left mouse button held down while dragging this copying handle.

The margins are shown for all the articles.

Third method:

1. Go to cell D9. Click on the Copy icon representing two pages. The cell is then surrounded by flashing dots.

2. Select the range D10:D12.

3. Validate.

The margins are shown for all the articles.

Figure 5.8: Copying a formula using the Copy icon

Relative references

In all three cases, Excel copies the basic formula contained in cell D9.

At the time of copying, the references of the initial formula are automatically adjusted.

When do we talk about relative references? Do the following exercise.

- Go to cells D10, D11 and D12 successively.
- Observe the formula bar.
- The initial formula B9 - C9 becomes B10 - C10, B11 - C11 and B12 - C12.

In this way, each formula always refers to the two cells preceding it on the same line, i.e. the sale price and the cost price of the corresponding article.

To achieve this, Excel has simply added to each reference of the initial formula a number of lines corresponding to the copying position with respect to this original formula.

Absolute references

The cell constitutes an absolute reference when its address does not depend on the position of the formula, but is defined absolutely by its line and column references on your spreadsheet.

For example, let us calculate the profit of the Grafico company.

The formula for calculating the profit made is:

Profit made on one article = Margin achieved on the article * quantity sold

To find the profit achieved:

1. Go to cell F9.
2. Select the range F9:F12.

3. Type the formula =D9*E9. The profit achieved on the sale of chalk is displayed in the cell.

4. Pull on the handle in the shape of a black cross to copy the calculation. The profit achieved for the other articles is displayed in cells F10, F11 and F12.

The formula for calculating the share of profit is:

Share of profit on an article = Profit achieved on the article / total profit

1. Go to G9, share of profit, then type =.

2. Click on F9, then type /.

3. Click on F14, the total profit achieved. Once the value is obtained (in our example '0.269'), copy the formula for the other three articles.

4. Select the range G9:G12, then copy the formula for the other three articles. You find that the error value #DIV/0! appears in the three cells.

Figure 5.9: The error message appears in the three cells

On going to these three cells, you find that on each occasion the initial formula is modified in the formula bar. For example, cell G11

informs us that formula F11 is divided by F16. Now F16 is an empty cell, and the default value of an empty cell is zero. By means of the error message, Excel is telling you that you are trying to divide by zero.

Unless the three precise formulae are entered in each of the cells, the initial formula G9 must be modified in order for the reference to the total profit achieved, F14, not to change on copying.

Cell F11 must therefore constitute an absolute reference in formula G9, that is a cell whose address does not depend on the position of the formula but is defined absolutely by its line and column references on your spreadsheet.

CALCULATING AN AVERAGE

Once again, our Grafico chart will serve as an example.

To calculate the average margin, follow the steps below.

1. Go to cell C18.

2. Type =, then Average.

3. Open brackets.

4. Select the range D11: D14.

5. Close brackets.

6. Confirm by pressing Enter.

Arguments must be numbers, names, matrices or references containing numbers. If a matrix or a reference typed as argument contains text, logical values or empty cells, these values are not taken into account. However, cells containing the value zero are taken into account.

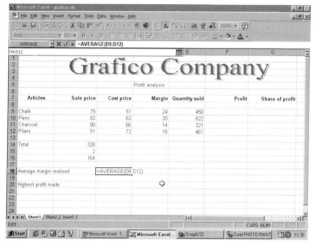

Figure 5.10: Calculating an average

CALCULATING AN AVERAGE USING THE FUNCTION WIZARD

To calculate an average using the Function Wizard, select the Fx icon called 'Paste a function'. The Function Wizard appears.

To use the Function Wizard, proceed as follows.

1. Click on the Average option.

2. Select the range over which you want to calculate the average in the dialog box above the Number 1. This is the range D9:D12.

3. Confirm by pressing Enter.

In our example, the result obtained is 19.

Excel 97

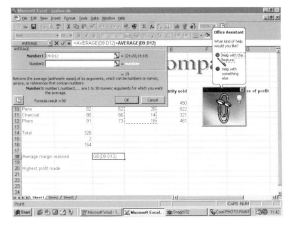

Figure 5.11: Calculating an average using the Function Wizard.

USING MATRIX FORMULAE

Imagine that you had to fix a sale price which would bring you the greatest profit. If you increase the price of your product too much, you will sell less. If you drop the price, you will sell more. A matrix calculation using Excel enables you to optimise your profits.

What is a matrix formula?

The matrix formula operates on two sets of values called matrix arguments.

Each matrix argument must have the same number of lines and columns. You create matrix formulae in the same way as simple standard formulae, as follows.

1. Select the cells which are going to contain the formula.

2. Create the formula.

3. Press Ctrl+Caps+Enter to type the formula.

84

Hour 6

Managing cells

THE CONTENTS FOR THIS HOUR

- Moving cells
- Copying cells
- Copying a string increased by increments
- Protecting cells
- Naming a range of cells
- Finding data
- Replacing data
- Accessing data
- Correcting data
- Sorting data

MOVING CELLS

Using the Clipboard

The first method of moving cells is to use the Clipboard.

1. Select the group of cells to be moved.

2. Click on the Edit menu.

3. Click on Cut.

4. Place the active cell at its intended destination.

5. Click on the Edit menu.

6. Click on Paste or on Insert and paste:

- The Paste option superimposes the cells moved in the destination cells.

- The Insert and paste option inserts the cells moved by pushing the old destination cells downwards or to the right.

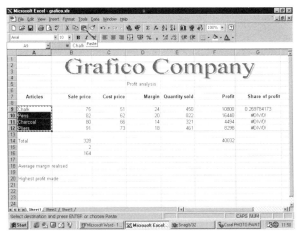

Figure 6.1: The Paste option superimposes the cells moved in the destination cells

Using the mouse

The mouse cursor takes the shape of an arrow when it is placed on the edge of the selection zone. By clicking the mouse button and dragging you can move the selection zone to where you want it.

COPYING CELLS

Using the Clipboard

The method is the same as for moving cells.

1. Select the cells to be copied.

2. Click on the Edit menu.

3. Click on Copy.

4. Place the active cell at its intended destination.

5. Click on the Edit menu.

6. Click on Paste or on Insert and paste.

By default, Excel copies all the attributes of the source cells. In order to copy only some of the attributes, click on the Edit menu and select Special paste, which allows you to select the attributes to be copied. To copy the content of the Clipboard to non-contiguous zones, select these zones beforehand.

Using the mouse

Hold the Ctrl button down while moving the mouse cursor, which turns into an arrow, to the edge of the selection zone. Still holding the Ctrl button down, click and drag the selection.

COPYING A STRING INCREASED BY INCREMENTS

▬▬▬ What is a string increased by increments?

A string increased by increments is a string of words or numbers with a logical sequence. For example:

- 1, 2, 3, 4, 5
- 3, 6, 9, 12
- Monday, Tuesday, Wednesday

▬▬▬ Copying a string increased by increments

You can automatically copy several types of string by selecting the cells and dragging the copying handle or using the String command.

1. To select the type of string, determine the starting value, e.g. 'Monday'.

2. Hold down the right mouse button and drag the copying handle.

▬▬▬ Creating a custom list

Text may be incremented if the list is created by the user, or if it represents names of months, days, etc. To access this custom list:

- Click on the Tools menu.
- Select Options.
- Click on the Custom lists tab.
- Enter the new string that you want to increment.

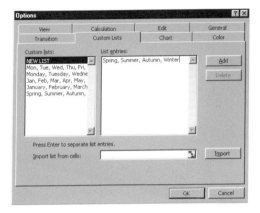

Figure 6.2: Creating your string increased by increments from the Options dialog box

PROTECTING CELLS

It is an easy matter to modify the content of cells consisting of constants or formulae.

It is simple to rewrite a constant. Rewriting a complex formula is more difficult. Therefore, the data must be protected. Excel is equipped with a system to protect work sheets which makes it possible to prevent undesirable alterations.

To start with, all cells are Locked.

To access this setting:

• Click on the Format menu.

• Select Cells.

• Click on the Protection tab.

The Cell Format dialog box tells you that locking is useless if the work sheet is not protected.

Figure 6.3: Check the 'Locked' box to lock the cell

To protect the work sheet, this is what you must do:

1. Click on the Tools menu.

2. Select the Protection submenu.

3. Select Protect Sheet.

Figure 6.4: The Protect Sheet option of the Tools menu

A dialog box opens on screen. Enter a password, e.g. 'Oxymoron'.

Figure 6.5: Entering your password

To confirm this password, rewrite it in the second dialog box in an identical manner.

If you forget your password, it will be impossible to recover it. We advise that you write it in a list of passwords which you keep in a safe place and that you distinguish lower case from upper case letters when entering it.

All the cells of your work sheet are now protected against being overwritten.

If you try to modify the content of one of the cells, Excel 97 then displays the following warning with an explanation of how to lift the protection:

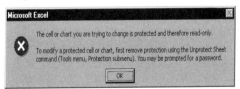

Figure 6.6: Warning against modifying a locked cell

Unprotect

To remove protection, proceed as follows:

1. Click on the Tools menu.

2. Select Protection.

3. Click on Unprotect.

A dialog box entitled Unprotect Sheet appears. Enter your password.
You can now write again in all the cells of your work sheet.

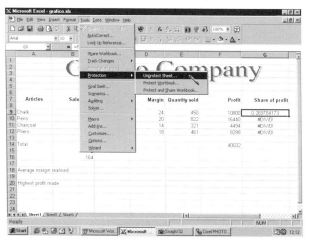

Figure 6.7: The Unprotect option

Figure 6.8: The Unprotect Sheet dialog box

Naming a range of cells

Allocating a name

The normal row – column references are not particularly simple to use in formulae, especially when cells are far away from the reference grid.

Excel allows the user to allocate a name to a cell or zone of cells. These names may be used instead of the references in all routine operations.

To name a range of cells:

1. Select the range of cells D7:D12 with the column header 'Margin'.

2. Click on the Insert menu.

3. Select Name.

4. Click on Define.

Figure 6.9: Typing the name 'Margin' in the text zone of the Define Name dialog box

The Name in the work book is Margin and corresponds to the range of cells D7:D12.

Rather than referring to the zone by the values D7:D12, you can designate it by its name: Margin.

Using names

A cell name may replace its reference in all calculation or reference operations. Just enter the name of the cell or the zone instead of its address.

To use a name:

1. Click on the drop-down list located to the right of the address of the current cell.

2. Select the name that you want from the list.

3. Use the commands Insert Name Paste.

For example, suppose cell A3 contains the value 180 and bears the name Credit, cell B3 contains the value 50 and bears the name Debit and that cell C3 is to contain the result and bears the name Balance.

1. Go to C3.

2. Instead of entering the formula = A2-B2, enter = Credit - Debit.

Figure 6.10: Carrying out an operation based on names

Allocating a name to a formula

When defining a name, it is possible to enter a complete expression in the box Refers to. This makes it possible to use this name instead of the formula. For example, in all formulae it is possible for VAT to be automatically replaced by 17.5%. The formula
= L (5) C* VAT
will hence become
L (5) C* 17.5.

Figure 6.11: The Refers to dialog box

ACCESSING DATA

Let us suppose that you want to go to the range of cells D7:D12 which you have named Margin:

1. Click on the Edit menu.

2. Click on Go to. A dialog box opens, showing the name which you have already given to the range D7:D12, Margin.

3. Confirm the choice. The Margin range is selected in your chart.

The functions Search, Replace and Go to are particularly useful when carrying out searches and making changes to long documents.

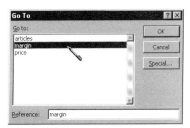

Figure 6.12: The Go to function

FINDING DATA

Use the following method to update data, text or numbers in a spreadsheet:

1. Click on Edit.

2. Select Find.

3. Type the text or number to be found in the dialog box. For example, let us suppose that it is the word 'Charcoal', located

in cell A11, at the intersection of row 11 and column A.

4. Confirm the choice.

Your selection box indicates the word 'Charcoal' to be found.

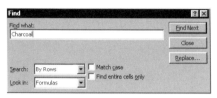

Figure 6.13: The Find function of the Edit menu

REPLACING DATA

Let us imagine that you want to replace the word 'Charcoal' by the word 'Crayons' in your chart for the Grafico company.

1. Click on Edit.

2. Select Find.

3. Complete the dialog box by typing 'Charcoal' in the Find what box.

4. Click on the Find Next button.

5. Type 'Crayons' in the Replace with box.

6. Click on Replace.

Figure 6.14: Find and Replace functions of the Edit menu

Excel 97 locates the word 'Charcoal' and replaces it with the new word. The word 'Crayons' appears in the chart of the Grafico company.

CORRECTING DATA

Use the following method to correct data.

1. Click on Tools.

2. Click on Spelling.

3. You can also click on the icon for this command, represented by ABC.

The Spelling button is indicated by the letters ABC underlined by a tick. Excel can check the spelling of the active document, the file or the work book.

The spellchecker proceeds to check the spelling of the Grafico chart.

No mistake has been made in the text, but the word Grafico is indicated as not being found in the dictionary.

You can ignore this comment or add the word to the dictionary.

You decide to add to your dictionary by clicking on Add.

Write the word 'Pliers' incorrectly, replacing the 'e' by 'a'.

Run the spellchecker on your chart.

The Automatic correction command automatically corrects the most common typing errors. Your word 'Pliars' is immediately located as not being found in the dictionary. In the dialog box, delete it and rewrite it correctly. Then click on Add. Your word reappears correctly in the chart.

Figure 6.15: The spellchecker checks the spelling of the content of cells

SORTING DATA

General principle

To sort data:

1. Select the zone to be sorted.

2. Click on Data.

3. Click on Sort.

4. Choose one, two or three sort keys in order of priority.

5. Use the click-and-drag technique.

Ascending order implies the following hierarchy:

- numbers

- text

- logical values

- empty cells

To sort data by alphabetical order you must first select the zone which you want to sort. If you want to classify articles by alphabetical order:

1. Select zone A7:F12.

2. Click on Data.

3. Click on Sort.

4. You can also use the AZ ascending sort icon.

The dialog box which appears on the screen asks you to validate an ascending sort for column A.

5. Confirm by clicking on OK.

The articles in your chart are classified in alphabetical order.

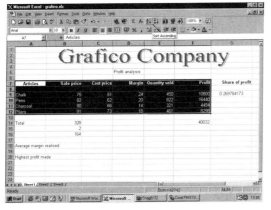

Figure 6.16: Sorting your data in alphabetical order

 Clicking on the Ascending sort icon has the effect of arranging the elements selected starting with the first letter of the alphabet, the smallest number or the earliest date. Sorting relates to the column containing the insertion point. If you have defined other sort options previously, these will still be valid.

Hour 7

Exploring advanced functions

THE CONTENTS FOR THIS HOUR

- Creating an outline
- Using an outline
- Consolidation
- Consolidation by category
- Consolidation by position
- Modifying a consolidation
- Creating a Pivot Table

CREATING AN OUTLINE

▬▬▬ What use is an outline?

An outline enables you to establish a hierarchy of rows or columns. To some extent it is the same principle as that used in dividing a book into chapters and paragraphs. It is possible just to show overall results in the spreadsheet without any details, as in the contents page of a book. An outline may be created automatically or manually.

You have four icons:

- **Outline symbols:** creates and displays the outline symbols on the spreadsheet. If the symbols are already displayed in an existing outline, clicking on the Display outline symbols icon will hide them.

- **PivotTable Report:** starts the PivotTable Wizard which guides you in creating or modifying a Pivot table.

- **Disassociate:** deletes the rows or columns selected within a spreadsheet group in outline mode. In a Pivot table this command disassociates each occurrence of a group, re-establishing the original individual elements of this group. For example, quarters are divided into original individual dates.

- **Group:** defines the rows or columns of detailed data which you have selected as a group forming part of an outline, in order for you to be able to summarise them. If you have not created an outline, this command creates one for you. In a Pivot table this command groups elements by category in order to create a single element from several elements. For example, you can group days, weeks, months or other dates in the form of quarters in order to carry out an analysis, to prepare a graph or to print out.

Excel 97 uses calculation formulae to try to determine the outline hierarchy.

If the spreadsheet is well structured, this method gives good results.

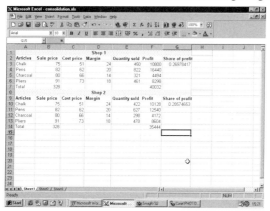

Figure 7.1: The structure of your chart

Automatic Outlining

1. Select the chart that you want to present in outlined form.

2. Click on Data.

3. Select Group and create an outline.

4. Click on Auto Outline.

You see immediately that there are two levels of outline in our example.

Vertical outline:

- sales by town

- sales by country

Horizontal outline:

- sales per month

- sales per quarter

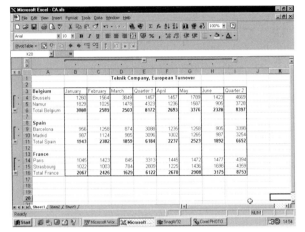

Figure 7.2: Your outline is created automatically

Your outline allows you to create a table which summarises the spreadsheet data.

- To expand or collapse outline levels, click on the Plus and Minus icons

- To display outline levels, click on buttons 1 and 2

Manual outlining

Select the highest hierarchical position to finish with the lowest, each time dropping by one selection in the previous hierarchy using the Group button.

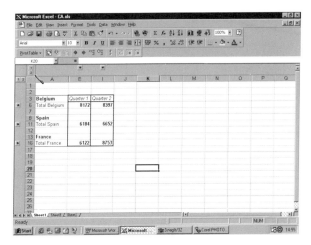

Figure 7.3: Your table presented in its most concise form

Using an outline

The Display outline symbols icon displays:

- the levels bars

- the expand (+) and collapse (-) buttons

- the line 1 and 2 level buttons.

Visible and invisible cells

When an outline is collapsed, displaying only the principal hierarchies (in our example, totals by country and by quarter), and the selected range is copied invisible cells are also copied or represented.

To remedy this:

1. Select the range of cells after hiding the lower hierarchies.

2. Click on the Select visible cells button.

Changing style

There are many predefined styles for the various outlines.

To select another style:

1. Click on Data.

2. Click on Group and create an outline.

3. Select Options.

4. Check the Automatic styles box.

5. Click on the Create button.

It is possible for you to modify these styles in the same way as the other data:

1. Click on Format.

2. Select the Styles command.

3. Click on the Modify button.

Figure 7.4: The Parameters dialog box and its Create styles option

CONSOLIDATION

Using your Excel 97 spreadsheet program you are going to be able to consolidate several spreadsheets.

You are going to consolidate data, e.g. the profit on the sale of graphic materials for the two shops of the Grafico parent company.

1. Make two tables which look the same.

2. Enter the data. The quantities sold and the profit achieved differ from one shop to the other.

3. Name your two new sheets Shop 1 and Shop 2.

In the example, we present them to you on one sheet, but you must record them on different sheets.

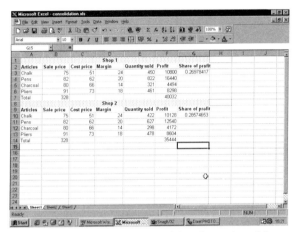

Figure 7.5: The profits achieved by shops 1 and 2

4. Open another spreadsheet.

5. Rename this spreadsheet Summary.

6. Copy the invariable data of the table, i.e. articles, sale price, cost price.

7. Leave the Quantity sold, Profit and Share of profit columns empty.

8. Click on Data.

9. Click on Consolidate. The drop-down Function list offers various consolidation options. Select those most used in your Shop 1 and Shop 2 tables (in this case, Sum, since you want to consolidate the profits of the two shops. But you could also add Maximum, Minimum or Product. The source worksheets of shops 1 and 2, called Grafico1 and Grafico 2, need not necessarily be opened.

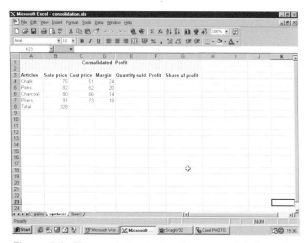

Figure 7.6: The worksheet showing consolidation of profits

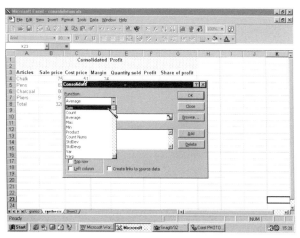

Figure 7.7: The Consolidate dialog box

10. Select the destination zone in the worksheet entitled Summary which is to receive the consolidation. This zone is F4:F7, that of the consolidated profit of shops 1 and 2.

11. Click on Data.

12. Select Consolidate.

13. Select the type of consolidation (sum, product, average, etc.).

14. Click in the Reference box and type the source zone for shop 1 or select it yourself in one of the workbook sheets.

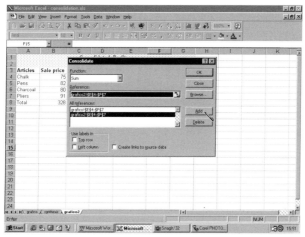

Figure 7.8: Source references in the Consolidate dialog box

15. Click on Add.

16. Repeat the operation for all source zones (in this example, you have only two).

17. Click on OK to carry out consolidation.

The consolidation calculations immediately appear in your Consolidated profit worksheet.

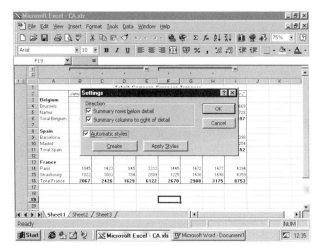

Figure 7.9: The consolidation calculations appear in your Consolidated profit table

If you check the Link to source data box, you can import all the detailed data of the source zones, but a generated outline will hide them. Without a link, Excel consolidates only the final values.

CONSOLIDATION BY CATEGORY

This method is useful when data to be consolidated do not occupy the same range of cells on their respective worksheet (which was not the case in the example given) but do have a common title.

It is easy to include titles in the source and destination zones and this will enable Excel to find the zones in question at the time of consolidation.

CONSOLIDATION BY POSITION

This method is useful when data to be consolidated are all in the same position throughout the source worksheets (as was the case in our example). It is not necessary to include titles in zone definitions.

MODIFYING A CONSOLIDATION

You have only to select another type of consolidation (Average, Minimum, Maximum, etc.) from the drop-down list of consolidation functions in order for Excel immediately to carry out new operations in the consolidation zone.

To remove a source zone:

1. Select the zone to be deleted.
2. Click on Delete.

To add a source zone:

1. Select the Source box.
2. Enter the new references.
3. Click on Add.
4. Click on Delete.

CREATING A PIVOT TABLE

▬▬▬ What is PivotTable?

PivotTable is a tool which makes it possible to present quickly, simply and efficiently the same table in different ways. If you are using a large complex table it is possible that different people consulting it will look for different information.

For example, let us imagine a class consisting of five pupils to whom three subjects are taught: French, mathematics and English.

Depending on whether the table is aimed at the pupils, their parents or their teachers, the approach will be different. The table must provide different information. This diversity of approach is what makes the table dynamic.

- Parents will want to read all the notes on their child easily, and then to compare them with those of the other pupils.

- Teachers will be interested mainly in their own subject.

- Pupils will in most cases be interested only in their own results.

The larger a table is, the more time PivotTable Wizard will save. Using this tool, and without modifying data, you will be able to produce different presentations suited to each party concerned. Better still, you will be able to carry out processing specific to each presentation. In fact, PivotTable offers summary results which can be reworked and sorted on demand, before transforming them into a graphic presentation.

For example, pupils may be sorted:

- by alphabetical order

- by overall results

- by averages in English

- by averages in French

- by averages in mathematics.

PivotTable allows you to allocate a document according to the information required. Data are entered once and presented several times.

The PivotTable toolbar

The PivotTable toolbar is presented as follows:

- **Disassociate:** in PivotTable mode this command disassociates each element of a group, re-establishing the original individual elements of this group. Example: quarters are divided into original individual dates.

- **Group:** in PivotTable mode, this command groups elements by category in order to create a single element from several elements. For example, days, weeks and months may be grouped in the form of quarters.

- **PivotTable Wizard:** guides you stage by stage in setting up and running a pivot table.

- **Dynamic field:** in PivotTable mode, this is a field on which you can act directly or indirectly.

- **Select labels:** in PivotTable mode, this command only selects labels when you click on a dynamic field label and not the associated data.

- **Select data:** in PivotTable mode, this command only selects data when you click on dynamic field data and not the associated labels.

- **Select data and labels:** in PivotTable mode, this command only selects data and labels when you click on dynamic field labels.

Figure 7.10: PivotTable toolbar

Before using the PivotTable Wizard, you must first create your table and enter the data. Let us take the example of the class of five pupils and three subjects taught for the months of January, February and March.

1. Allocate marks out of 20 to each of the children.

2. Save your table.

3. Click on Data.

4. Select PivotTable Report.

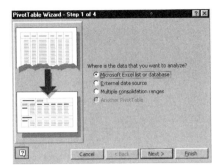

Figure 7.11: Stage 1 of creating your pivot table

Stage 2 of creating your pivot table involves selecting the range criteria that you want to match. This must include all column and row headers.

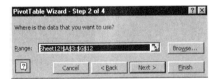

Figure 7.12: Stage 2 of creating your pivot table

Stage 3 requires that you create your pivot table by dragging the field buttons on the diagram.

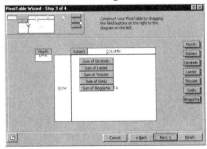

Figure 7.13: Stage 3 of creating your pivot table

During stage 4 you must choose whether to display the result on the same worksheet or on another. If you want to produce customised graphs for each new pivot table, you should opt for a separate worksheet.

Figure 7.14: Stage 4 of creating your pivot table

You have now created your pivot table. It is now up to you to read it from whatever angle interests you.

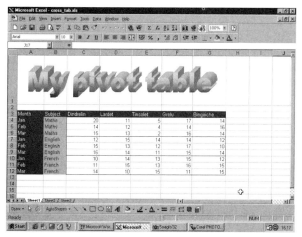

Figure 7.15: Your completed pivot table

By clicking on the list of subjects, you can obtain the averages for each course individually.

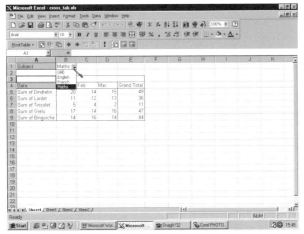

Figure 7.16: The results obtained in mathematics for each pupil

A pivot table may be compared with successive stacked worksheets which are instantly represented on a single worksheet. The basic principle consists of overlaying columns in order to represent the additional dimension. The pivot table will provide a clear presentation based on a complete but slightly muddled document. The Page heading allows you to reproduce the original stack. For example, if the Page heading corresponds to the month, by clicking on the drop-down list you will have all the results for a given month. If the page represents the Subject heading, the drop-down list will offer a summary table for the results in the subject chosen. If the Page heading is not completed, the table will be more complete but less easy to read.

Hour 8

Creating a database

THE CONTENTS FOR THIS HOUR

- Creating a database
- Using the data form
- Moving around a database
- Sorting a database
- Using filters

CREATING A DATABASE

What is a database?

A database is a tool allowing information to be managed, extracted and filtered and data to be calculated and analysed.

A database necessarily begins with a first line of description of the record structure. Data must start under the field name. Field names cannot contain punctuation marks or spaces.

There must be no homonyms.

Setting up a database

The Grafico company has a group of individuals as customers. The customer services manager wants to know the name of each customer, his or her telephone number and the value of his or her latest order.

These three headings (Name, Telephone No. and Last order) will constitute the structure, i.e. the *fields* of the database.

You are going to create this database, this list of information, on the spreadsheet.

First of all type the headings in the same row.

Enter the information carefully one row below the headings.

Each heading contains the same type of data.

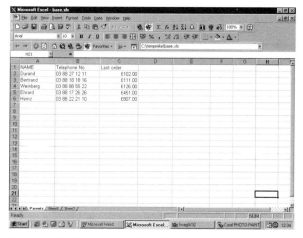

Figure 8.1: Entering the headings and data

Using the data form

The data entry form displays a form in a dialog box. You can use the data entry form to display, modify, add, delete and find records contained in a list or database.

The data entry form allows you to process a database's records:

1. Click on Data.

2. Click on Form.

Entering a record

To enter a record:

1. Place the cursor on the next row of the database.

2. Click on New.

3. Enter the data.

4. Click on New to validate the current record.

Figure 8.2: Data entry form dialog box

The entry is recorded after any previous entries.

Excel automatically enters all the fields of the database in the entry box. The software also offers various commands enabling you to move around the database, to add and delete records, use selection criteria, etc.

Customised formats

Excel has predefined formats to which you can add customised formats which you create yourself.

Customised formats are useful in order to specify the thousands separator, the number of decimal places, the currency symbol or the unit of measurement.

To access this Cell format dialog box:

1. Click on Format.

2. Select Cell.

3. Click on Number of cells.

The drop-down list will offer the following categories:

- **Standard:** cells with a standard format do not have any specific number format.

- **Number:** this category is used to display numbers in general. Clicking on it reveals a counter enabling you to adjust the decimal part of numbers, an option offering the use of thousand separators and another option enabling you to choose the presentation of negative numbers.

- **Currency:** currency formats are used for general currency values. The drop-down Symbol list gives you access to all international currency symbols.

- **Accountancy:** accountancy formats align currency symbols and decimals in a column.

- **Date:** date formats display date and time serial numbers as a date value. Use the hour formats to display only the time.

- **Time:** time formats display date and time serial numbers as a time value. Use date formats to display only the date.

- **Percentage:** percentage formats multiply the value of the cell by 100 and display the result with the percentage symbol.

- **Fraction:** fraction formats offer you fractions of one to three figures.

- **Text:** text format cells are treated as text even if they contain a number. The cell is displayed exactly as it has been entered.

- **Special:** special formats are used for list and database values.

- **Customised:** enter the code of the number format using one of the existing codes as starting point.

An example of a specific application of these various customised formats concerns the way in which you want to display telephone numbers in your database. Let us suppose that you have clients of different nationalities, UK and French, for example. The telephone numbers will be different.

To enter a telephone number in the French format:

1. Enter your telephone number, digit by digit, without worrying about its format.

2. Select it.

3. Click on the Format menu.

4. Click on Cell.

5. Click on Number.

6. Choose Special format.

7. Click on French Telephone number in the Type drop-down list.

8. Validate by clicking on OK.

Your telephone number appears in the database in French format.

For a telephone number in the French format, carry out the operation again, but this time selecting the option Telephone number from the Type drop-down list. You also find the options Belgium, Canada, Luxembourg, Morocco and Switzerland.

Adding a record

To add a record:

1. Click on New.

2. Click on Data.

3. Click on Form.

4. Select New.

5. Enter your new record.

Deleting a record

To delete a record:

1. Click anywhere in your database to activate it.

2. Click on Data.

3. Click on Form.

4. Select the record which you want to delete.

5. Click on Delete. A message appears on your screen to warn you that the record is going to be destroyed.

6. Confirm.

Figure 8.3: The Delete button in the data entry form dialog box

Finding a record

You can use the data entry form or the database to find a record.

Using the data entry form:

1. Activate your database by clicking anywhere on it.

2. Select Data and then Form.

3. Click on the Criteria option.

4. Enter the criteria which concern you, e.g. the order valued £451.00.

5. Click on Next to validate.

Your record appears in full.

Using the database:

Let us suppose that your database contains several hundred names. To find the record for 'Weinberg':

1. Click on Edit.
2. Select Find.
3. Type the name 'Weinberg' in the text box.
4. Confirm.

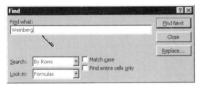

Figure 8.4: Entering the name in the Find dialog box

Criteria

The Criteria command of the data entry form dialog box finds records according to the criteria which you indicate.

Use the direction arrows in the dialog box to move from one record to another.

To jump 10 records at a time, click on the scrollbar between the arrows.

MOVING AROUND A DATABASE

You have two commands at your disposal in order to move around the database:

- **Previous:** displays the previous record in a list. If you indicate a criterion using the Criteria button, Previous displays the previous record meeting the criterion.

Excel 97

- **Next:** displays the next record in a list. If you indicate a criterion using the Criteria button, Next displays the next record meeting the criterion.

SORTING A DATABASE

▩▩▩▩ The Name field

You can sort your database according to numerical or alphabetical criteria.

1. Select your database.

2. Click on Data.

3. Click on Sort.

Figure 8.5: The Sort option of the Data menu

Select the option Ascending sort by names.

Figure 8.6: The dialog box allowing you to sort your list by alphabetical order

Your list of names is classified in alphabetical order.

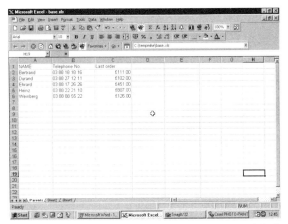

Figure 8.7: Your list is sorted by ascending alphabetical order

You can sort a small selection rather than the whole list.

Just select the names that you want to sort and click on Sort under the Data menu.

Last order field

To sort by orders:

1. Select your database.

Figure 8.8: Sorting your list by order value

2. Click on Data.

3. Click on Sort.

4. Activate Last order in the text box.

5. Validate by clicking on OK.

Your list is classified in ascending order by the value of the last order placed.

USING FILTERS

▬▬▬ AutoFilter

AutoFilter only displays the rows corresponding to the value of the active cell and inserts AutoFilter arrows to the right of each column label.

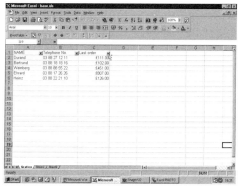

Figure 8.9: AutoFilter is activated

To activate AutoFilter:

1. Select the Data menu.

2. Select the Filter submenu.

3. Confirm.

To deactivate AutoFilter and recover the entire list:

1. Select the Data menu.

2. Select the Filter submenu.

3. Select Deactivate filter.

You can also select Show all.

Advanced Filter

The Advanced Filter filters the data of a list so that only those rows meeting a condition which you specify using a criteria range are displayed.

The Advanced Filter enables you to make a more complex selection based on different criteria concerning a single column. For example, you can apply three criteria to the Name column.

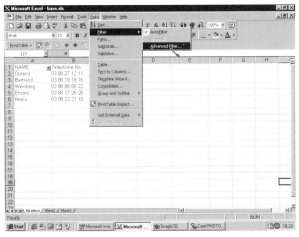

Figure 8.10: A dialog box appears in order for you to enter your criteria

To access the Advanced Filter:

1. Click on Data.

2. Select the Filter submenu.

3. Click on Advanced filter.

Figure 8.11: The Advanced Filter dialog box

Retrieving a record using AutoFilter

To retrieve a record:

1. Click anywhere on your database.

2. Click on Data.

3. Click on the Filter submenu.

4. Select AutoFilter.

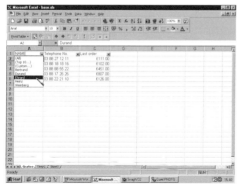

Figure 8.12: Sorting using the AutoFilter

Three drop-down menus then appear on your database, marked by a small black downwards arrow, each corresponding to one of the three headings.

Select the customer name corresponding to the record that you want to retrieve.

1. Click on Name.

2. Select 'Ehrard'.

3. Confirm.

Your database is filtered. Only the retrieved 'Ehrard' record appears.

To show the whole of your list:

1. Click on Data.

2. Select Filter.

3. Click on Show All.

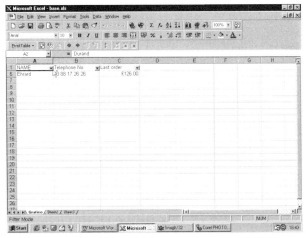

Figure 8.13: Only the 'Ehrard' record appears

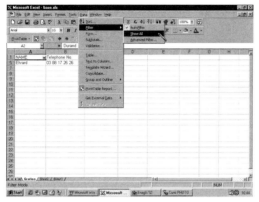

Figure 8.14: The Show All option enables you to see your entire list

Operators

The operators used to filter information are as follows:

=   The equals sign indicates exact correspondence.

>   The greater than sign indicates higher values.

<   The less than sign indicates lower values.

>=   The greater than or equal to sign indicates higher or equal values.

<=   The less than or equal to sign indicates lower or equal values.

<>   The different from sign indicates different values.

=   The equals sign on its own searches for all non-empty fields.

Clear Removes all criteria.

Hour 9

Creating a chart

THE CONTENTS FOR THIS HOUR

- Creating a chart
- Activating a chart
- Modifying a chart
- Changing the type of chart
- Moving a chart
- Modifying the series of a chart
- Formatting a chart

CREATING A CHART

Microsoft has considerably improved Excel 97's graphics package. Sophisticated features are now available. In addition to standard charts, you can now add radar, cylinders, pyramids and bubbles to your charts. All these geometric shapes are also offered in 3D.

One of the most notable new features of the updated Excel is the possibility of orienting charts and their legends through 0° to 180°.

Graphics packages are part and parcel of office automation, in the same way as word-processing or accounting software. They are used to complement the latter, for example, to give greater impact to advertising, annual accounts, balance sheets, etc.

They are of greatest use in presenting figures, which are often complex and difficult to interpret, in a clear, simple manner.

Before creating a chart to illustrate plain, coded and complex data, which is rendered immediately understandable, we will look at the tools which the user has for creating graphs.

Chart toolbar

The Chart toolbar is made up of different drop-down menus and icons:

- **Chart type:** changes the type of chart for a single data series, for a chart group or for an entire chart.

- **Source data:** adds or modifies the data series or data points selected in a chart.

- **Chart options:** modifies the standard options of the chart type that you select. You can rename charts, change the default parameters of gridlines and axes, change how data labels are displayed, etc.

- **Position:** organises the position of selected objects on the spreadsheet.

- **Add data:** adds selected data series or data points to the chart.

- **Add a trend curve:** adds trend curves or modifies the type of trend curve in the data series of surface charts, bar charts, histograms, line and scatter charts.

- **3D view:** controls the angle from which you see 3D effects. A sample chart, displayed in the dialog box, shows the current parameters.

- **Adjusted to window:** determines whether or not the size of the chart sheet depends on the size of the window. A chart sheet which has just been created is, by default, not dependent on the window size.

- **Chart window:** shows or hides the chart window.

- **Chart title format:** formats the chart title. The formatting options available vary depending on the chart component selected. If you select a legend, the option is called selected legend.

- **Chart Wizard:** the Chart Wizard guides you through all the stages of creating your chart. In four simplified stages it helps you to create high-quality charts.

- **Different chart types:** these include surface, bar, line, pie, scatter, donut, radar, bubble, pyramid, cone, cylinder charts.

- **Vertical gridlines:** shows or hides the vertical gridlines of charts.

- **Horizontal gridlines:** shows or hides the horizontal gridlines of charts.

- **Legend:** this command adds a legend to the right of the plot area or resizes it. If the chart already has a legend, clicking on this command deletes it.

- **Data table:** displays the values for each data series in a grid below the chart.

- **Series in rows:** plots the data series of the chart using data row by row.

- **Series in columns:** plots the data series of the chart using data column by column.

What is the best type of chart to use?

There are six main chart types.

- **Line charts:** line charts emphasise a trend, for example sales for the first quarter.

- **Surface charts:** these emphasise a total. They allow two very different variables to be compared. Surface charts are suited to highlighting the extent of a development, for example the margin realised month by month for the past year.

- **Bar charts:** vertical bar charts, otherwise known as 'histograms', are intended to present a classification, for example to present the company balance sheet over several years in terms of variations in staff, absenteeism and total wages and salaries. Stacked vertical bar charts are a variant on this theme and present a single vertical bar per point on the abscissa and superimpose the different values. This arrangement shows up the composition of several groups, for example the cost price component, or the division by article type of the turnover of representatives.

Do not overuse vertical bar charts or histograms! They play the role of 'catch-all'. For example, if you do not know what type of chart to use to illustrate your case study, the vertical bar chart could be your joker!

- **Pie charts:** these are recommended for emphasising proportions. They represent the ratio of parts to a whole. They are also used to indicate a distribution, for example the geographical distribution of a company's sales.

- **Scatter diagrams:** scatter diagrams or 'correlation charts' indicate a correlation, that is a relationship of cause and effect, for example of advertising costs to increased sales.

- **Specific charts:** these may be stock exchange graphs, age pyramids, etc.

Some types of chart may be combined. A single chart then presents several different charts, for example a histogram may be superimposed on a line chart to show the peaks of a particular series, the best or worst sales of a year, etc. However, take care not to overload your charts with information. Too much information is a bad thing as the message becomes vague.

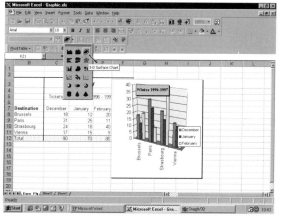

Figure 9.1: Chart toolbar

Why use 3D?

You can now choose between creating a chart in 3D or 2D. 3D has many uses, in addition to being more pleasing to the eye, as it is closer to reality.

Charts in 3D, i.e. in three dimensions, enable you to represent several series at the same time using perspective. In the case of charts in 3D, the vertical axis is the z axis. The name of data is still plotted along the x axis, but the name of the series is along the y axis and values are staggered along the z axis.

A histogram for the Euro Fly company

The Euro Fly company sells air tickets to European destinations. Let us suppose you want to show ticket sales by month and by destination. The period which concerns you most is winter 1996-97, namely December 1996, January 1997 and February 1997. The destinations are Brussels, Paris, Strasbourg and Vienna.

What type of chart do you choose to illustrate this case study?

The histogram is the standard solution as, in this relatively simple case study, first and foremost you are representing one classification.

To create a chart, first of all select the data that you want to include. Select the whole of the Euro Fly Table with the exception of the totals.

Click on the Chart Wizard icon on the Chart toolbar.

Stage 1

A menu opens on-screen. The first tab offers a choice of standard charts and subcharts, and the second tab offers a choice of customised charts.

Figure 9.2: Your data as it appears before being made into a chart

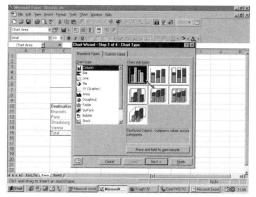

Figure 9.3: Choose a chart in the form of a histogram

The chart best suited to the data in our table is the straightforward histogram. Click on Next.

Stage two

Your data range offers you a series in rows or columns. Let us say you choose the series in columns which you feel is most legible. Click on Next.

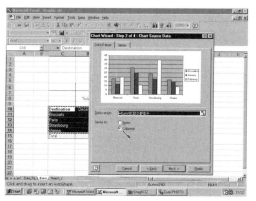

Figure 9.4: Choosing the series in columns

Stage three

A choice of options is offered which will make your chart even easier to read.

· titles to be given

· axes to be shown

· gridlines to be shown

· legend to be added

Enter the title Winter 96–97 and click on Next.

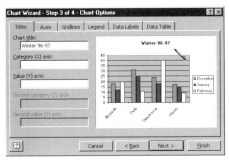

Figure 9.5: Entering your title, Winter 96–97

Stage four

You are given the choice of embedding this chart in a new worksheet or as an object in the worksheet which includes your data. Check the box As object in Euro.

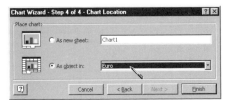

Figure 9.6: Fourth and final stage

Click on End. Your chart is embedded in your worksheet. You now only have to adapt its size to the space available on the worksheet. To do this, use the small black resizing blocks surrounding the chart framework.

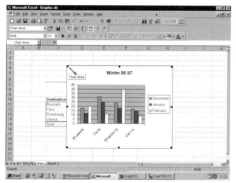

Figure 9.7: Adapting the size of your chart to the space available on the worksheet

ACTIVATING A CHART

To activate a chart, double-click inside its frame. The frame is surrounded by a dark border.

Figure 9.8: To activate your chart, double-click inside the frame

MODIFYING A CHART

Once your chart has been activated you will be able to make any changes you want.

For example, you can change the font.

1. Click on the chart title and it is activated immediately.

2. Click on the Format chart title icon.

3. Select the Book Antiqua font in 12 point size.

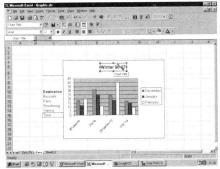

Figure 9.9: Activate the title of your chart by double-clicking on it

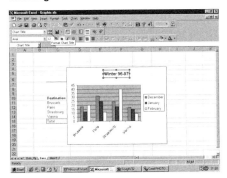

Figure 9.10: The Format chart title icon enables you to format the title

CHANGING THE TYPE OF CHART

Do you feel that the histogram chart is not clear enough?

If your prefer a bar chart:

1. Click on the chart to activate it.

2. Select the Chart Type icon. You are offered 18 chart types.

3. Select the Bar type.

MOVING A CHART

To move a chart:

1. Click on your chart.

2. Drag it to where you want it.

A dotted frame indicates the size of your graphic object.

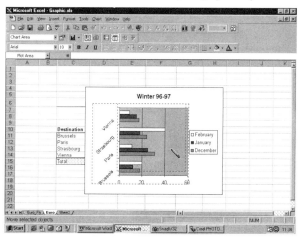

Figure 9.11: Move your chart inside the frame

MODIFYING THE SERIES OF A CHART

1. Click on your chart to activate it.

2. Select the Source Data submenu from the Chart menu.

Clicking on the Series tab opens a dialog box where you can write the name of the series which you want to add or delete.

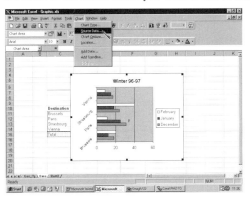

Figure 9.12: The Chart menu with the Source data option

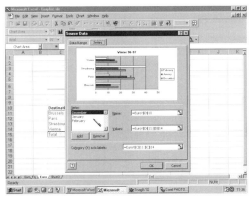

Figure 9.13: Entering the name of the series to be added in the Series box

FORMATTING A CHART

▇▇▇ Simple format

For a simple chart format:

1. Click on your chart to activate it.

2. Select the Format Plot Area icon.

3. Choose a colour which is not too striking and which matches the colours of the Euro Fly company to fill your plot area.

In the same way, you can add a shadow to your title:

1. Click on the title to activate it.

2. Click on the Format Chart Title icon.

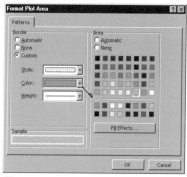

Figure 9.14: The Format Plot Area dialog box for formatting your chart

Select a customised border and shadow for your title.

To format your numerical data, avoid using red. This colour has a negative connotation. Moreover, try to use colours close to those of the company's logo in order to remain in keeping with it and make your chart pleasing to the eye.

3D format

Why do without 3D when it exists? With increasingly sophisticated design software and graphics packages, the aesthetic requirements of users and above all readers are increasingly demanding. Do not hesitate to present your chart as well as you can, while remembering that the most important thing is to convey your message clearly.

1. Click on your chart.

2. Select your Chart Wizard.

3. Select the cylinder option.

4. Validate.

5. Click on the corners of your new chart to angle it.

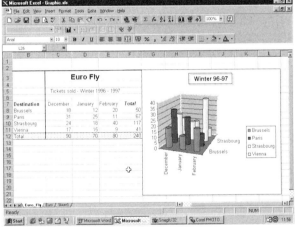

Figure 9.15: Your chart in 3D

Hour 10

Creating a macro

THE CONTENTS FOR THIS HOUR

- Creating a macro
- Recording a macro
- Displaying a macro
- Copying a macro
- Editing a macro
- Assigning a macro to a toolbar
- Changing the image of a macro button
- Editing a button
- Macro virus protection

Some tasks require a succession of operations which never varies. They are repetitive. To automate a repetitive task it is possible to create a specific worksheet, known as a macro worksheet. This macro must contain all the actions to be carried out automatically, in the order in which they are executed. You can allocate it to a button on the toolbar.

CREATING A MACRO

Macro tools

Before creating your own macros, it is best to get to know the macro tools which Excel 97 offers.

The Tools menu offers two options relating to macros:

- Macros
- Add-Ins

The Macros option

The Macros option opens a Macro dialog box.

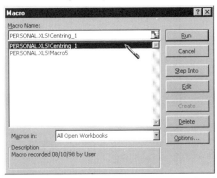

Figure 10.1: The Macro dialog box in the Tools menu

This dialog box contains the following drop-down lists and commands.

- **Macro name:** the Macro Name box allows you to write the name of the macro which you want to create, edit or delete, or for which you want to define options.

- **Run:** the Run command runs the macro selected. If a macro contains arguments (variables) you cannot run it from the Macro dialog box.

- **Step Into:** the Step Into command runs the macro selected code line by code line.

- **Edit**: this opens the macro selected in Visual Basic Editor, a window collection dedicated to debugging macros. You then go into Visual Basic programming mode.

- **Create:** this opens a new sequence in Visual Basic Editor. This command button is only available if you type a new name in the Macro Name box.

- **Delete:** this deletes the macro selected.

- **Options:** the Options button opens up a new dialog box which gives the macro selected a shortcut key consisting of Ctrl + the letter that you type.

- **Description:** this text box enables you to add information relating to the macro to facilitate its use.

Figure 10.2: The Macro Options dialog box

The Add-Ins option

This option opens up a dialog box called Add-Ins. It comprises:

- A drop-down list containing the programs available in Excel 97, which are at the same time sophisticated macros and complete programs. The best known of these is Solver. It solves equations according to the constraints which you enter. For example, one may wish to find how to spend more while earning less. Solver does not always find an answer, but it is, in this case, precise enough to state that the problem posed does not strictly allow for any solution.

- A file conversion wizard.

Just check a box to load an add-in and make it available in Excel. If you want to unload an additional macro and free up memory, deactivate the checked box.

Figure 10.3: Add-Ins dialog box

RECORDING A MACRO

Before recording a macro, it is strongly recommended to prepare its work and plan its stages. In fact, if you make the smallest error while recording the macro, the corrections which you make are also recorded.

Do not confuse recording and running a macro. Recording makes it possible to indicate to Excel its different actions. Running a macro consists of activating it.

▬▬ First example

1. Click on Tools.

2. Select macro.

3. Click on Record New Macro.

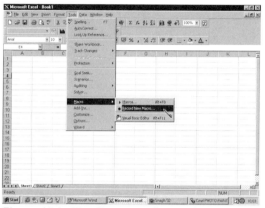

Figure 10.4: The first stage in creating a macro

4. Enter the name that you want to give to your macro in the text box of the dialog box.

5. Confirm by clicking on OK. It is preferable to choose a short name which comprises only letters.

Figure 10.5: Your macro is called Centring.FHV

6. Carry out the operations involved in creating your macro.

7. When the process is completed, click on Tools.

8. Click on the Macro submenu.

9. Select the Stop Recording option.

Your macro is completed.

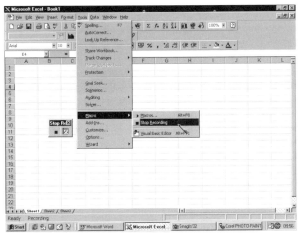

Figure 10.6: The Stop Recording option

To stop a macro before recording is completed, press ESC.

Second example

To familiarise yourself with creating macro commands, you are going to create a general purpose macro. It consists of centring the title of the spreadsheet, or one of its paragraphs, horizontally, vertically and over several columns (merging cells).

To do this:

1. Write your text. In this example, it will be 'My beautifully centred title'.

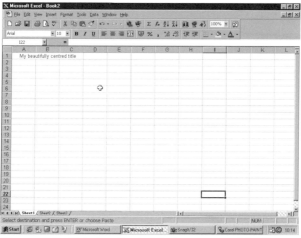

Figure 10.7: Entering the text to be processed by the macro

2. Select the entire area where the text is to be centred, starting with the text cell.

3. From there only, click on Tools, Macro, Record New Macro.

Name the macro Centring_1.

Figure 10.8: Giving a name to your macro

4. Confirm. The macro recording symbol appears, with two buttons:

- Relative reference

- Stop recording

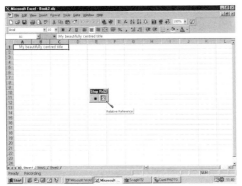

Figure 10.9: The Relative Reference button of the Macro toolbar

1. Click on Format Cells.

2. Select the Alignment tab.

3. Under Horizontal and Vertical select Center.

4. Select the Merge cells checkbox.

5. Confirm. The text is displayed centred as you wish.

6. Click on the stop button (the first of the two).

Assigning a macro to a toolbar

1. Click with the right mouse button on any toolbar.

Instead of activating a command, this operation gives access to a drop-down menu.

2. Select Customize.

3. Click on the Commands tab.

4. Click on Macros.

5. Place the customised button on the toolbar.

6. Click with the right mouse button on the *smiley*.

7. Select the Edit button command.

8. Modify the button representing centring.

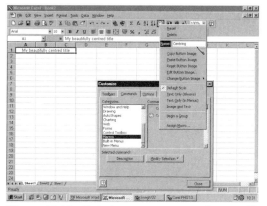

Figure 10.10: Entering your command name 'Centring' in the text box in order for it to appear in the information bubble

9. Close the windows which are no longer being used.

10. Click on the new button.

11. In the dialog box which appears, select the macro Centring_1.

The new tool is now ready to run. It is efficient, clear and functional.

You can test it.

1. Enter a title at random.

2. Select it.

3. Click on your Centring macro.

In order for a macro to select a specific cell, execute an action, then select another cell in correlation with the active cell, mix up absolute references and relative references during recording.

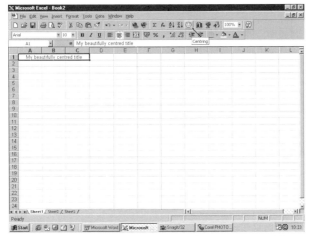

Figure 10:11: Your macro with its Smiley icon and its Centring information bubble

The Relative Reference option enables you to record a macro using relative references. Not clicking on the Relative Reference option enables you to record a macro using absolute references.

DISPLAYING A MACRO

To display a macro:

1. Click on Tools.

2. Select the Macro submenu.

3. Click on Macro.

4. Click on the Step Into button.

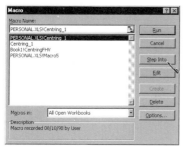

Figure 10.12: The Step Into command button for displaying your macro

You obtain on screen a breakdown of your macro operations.

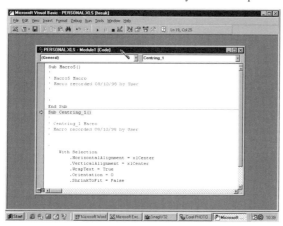

Figure 10.13: Your macro displayed

COPYING A MACRO

There may be commands in the syntax of an initial macro which you want to assign to another macro. You can copy all or part of the first macro to another. You can also copy a macro module in order to duplicate all the macros stored in it.

Copying part of a macro

1. Click on Tools.

2. Click on Macros.

3. Enter the name of the macro to be copied in the Name box.

4. Click on the Modify button.

5. Select the segments of the macro that you want to copy.

If you want to copy everything, you must include the lines Sub and End Sub in the selection.

1. Click on Copy.

2. Open the module in which you want to insert this copy.

3. Click on Paste.

Copying a macro module

1. Select Macros from the Tools menu.

2. Click on the Display Visual Basic Editor menu.

3. Click on Explorer.

4. Drag the module that you want to copy to the destination workbook.

EDITING A MACRO

You have made a mistake in your macro's sequence of operations. You want to correct it.

1. Click on Tools.

2. Click on Macro.

3. Select Edit.

The syntax of your macro appears on screen. You can edit it as you wish.

ASSIGNING A MACRO TO A TOOLBAR

1. Click on View.

2. Select the Toolbars submenu.

3. Click on Customize.

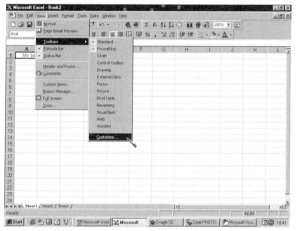

Figure 10.14: The Customize option of the toolbar for customising your macro button

4. Click on the Commands tab.

5. Select Macros.

6. Click on the Custom button.

7. Drag it to the place where you want it on the toolbar, holding down the left button of your mouse.

The cursor becomes a white arrow on a small grey rectangular command button.

Figure 10.15: Dragging your macro button to where you want it on the toolbar

8. Drop the macro where you want it on your toolbar by releasing the left mouse button. The custom macro button is now positioned in the middle of the toolbar.

CHANGING THE IMAGE OF A MACRO BUTTON

To change the image of your macro's button:

1. Click on View.

2. Select Toolbars.

3. Click on Customize.

4. Select your custom macro button.

5. Click on Change Button Image.

6. Select the new button image. You can choose between 42 new icons. If you do not like any of them, you can create one yourself.

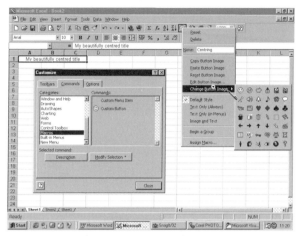

Figure 10.16: Choosing an icon from the forty two offered

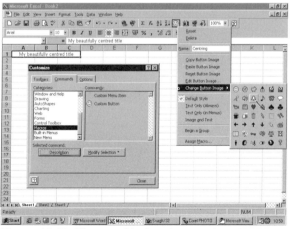

Figure 10.17: The new Big Ben icon assigned to your macro

Your new icon takes is position on the toolbar.

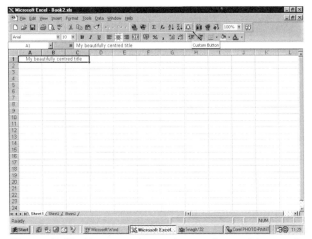

Figure 10.18: Your new icon takes up its position on the toolbar

Now you can create any button you want.

EDITING A BUTTON

You can create buttons yourself and make any changes to them that you feel are necessary.

These are the various operations which you must carry out.

1. Click on View.

2. Select Toolbars.

3. Click on Customize.

4. Select your custom macro button.

5. Click on Modify selection.

6. Click on the Edit Button Image.

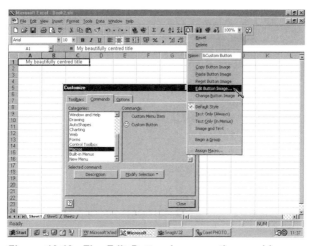

Figure 10.19: The Edit Button Image option enables you to fashion your icon

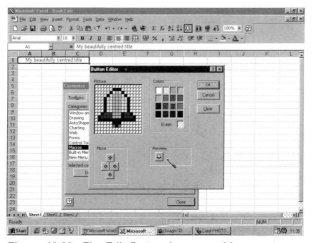

Figure 10.20: The Edit Button Image enables you to create your own icons

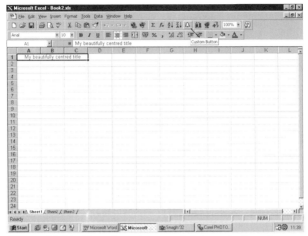

Figure 10.21: Your icon is completely redesigned

MACRO VIRUS PROTECTION

There are macro-specific viruses which Microsoft Excel does not detect. You must obtain macro antivirus protection software.

A macro virus is a virus stored in macros. When you execute an action which triggers a macro virus, this may become active and be placed in a hidden location.

If you want to know more about macro antivirus protection, do not hesitate to consult Microsoft's website. You can download all the information you need.

Hour 11

Connecting to the Internet

THE CONTENTS FOR THIS HOUR

- Selecting the Web toolbar
- Saving a document in HTML format
- Displaying a Web page using Netscape Navigator
- Creating a hyperlink
- Navigating on the Web
- Opening Favorites
- Going to the Start Page
- Putting URLs in the spreadsheet

With Office 97 you can now open workbooks on the Internet. You can create your own Web pages, access other files using hyperlinks, deposit your Excel files on the Internet, search the Internet for useful data and thus enrich your work.

For companies, subscription to the Internet offers the benefit of allowing a high volume of communications at low prices. Insofar as compression programs often reduce files by a ratio of 1:20, the Internet makes it possible to transfer data efficiently and quickly.

SELECTING THE WEB TOOLBAR

To select your Web toolbar:

1. Click on View.

2. Click on Toolbars.

3. Select Customize.

4. Click on Web.

The Web toolbar appears on the screen.

The Excel 97 Web toolbar allows you to access your Web documents (HTML, Jpeg, Gif and animated Gif format) on the hard disk (without connection) and on the network once a connection has been established.

It comprises the following icons.

- **Address**: in the Address text box, enter the Internet address that you want to call, or select an address already used from the list.

- **Open:** this opens the hyperlink.

- **Open Favorites:** this displays the folder in the Look in box. The Favorites folder contains shortcuts to files, folders and hyperlinks which are frequently used.

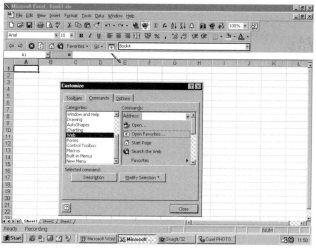

Figure 11.1: The various commands on the Web toolbar

- **Start Page:** you can define the start page using the Choose a start page command from the Go menu on the Web toolbar.

- **Search the Web:** this opens a search page on the Web. You can search for information, sites, etc. on the Web.

- **Go:** this displays a list of commands belonging to the category which you select in the box called Categories. To add a command to a toolbar, just drag the desired element from the Commands box to the toolbar.

- **Back:** this opens the previous file in the list containing the last 10 files consulted.

- **Stop search for link:** this stops the search for the link in progress.

- **Refresh active page:** this updates the selected active page, reloading it.

- **Add to favorites:** this creates a shortcut to the file, folder or link selected, then adds it to the Favorites folder. The original file or folder is not moved.

- **Display only Web toolbar:** this hides all toolbars displayed except for the Web toolbar. Just click again on this icon to show the hidden toolbars.

- **Insert/edit hyperlink:** this inserts or modifies the hyperlink specified.

- **Web toolbar:** this shows or hides the Web toolbar.

SAVING A DOCUMENT IN HTML FORMAT

What is HTML format?

HTML means Hypertext Markup Language. It is the file format used on the Web. First used to format text, this language has developed considerably. It allows sound, graphics, video and form files to be incorporated in sites. For this reason HTML is becoming the standard for creating pages on the Web.

An HTML file contains two categories of data:

- **The content:** the information that you want to show on your page. Let us suppose that it is a presentation site for your graphical works. You may, for instance, put down a few words of introduction, your biography and your scanned canvasses.

- **Markers**: these define text formatting and enrichment. In other words, markers represent the programming part of the page. They are invisible.

Saving in HTML format

Click on File and then on Save as HTML

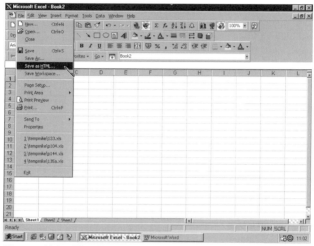

Figure 11.2: The File menu and its Save as HTML option

Step 1

The Internet Assistant Wizard guides you in converting your data and charts to Web pages in HTML format.

At this initial stage, you must select the ranges and charts which are to appear on the Web page.

All the charts in your workbook are listed.

To remove the ranges or charts which are not to be inserted in the Web page, click on the Delete button.

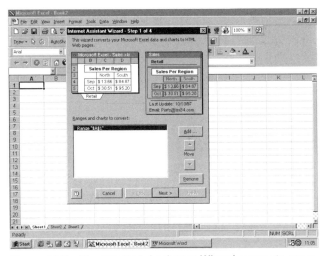

Figure 11.3: The Internet Assistant Wizard converts your data and charts to HTML format

Step 2

When you have reached this second stage, you must specify whether you want to create a Web page in HTML format or simply to copy your data to an existing Web page.

The Internet Assistant Wizard offers to convert your data in two different ways:

- You can create an independent ready-to-view HTML document that contains your formatted data.

- You can also insert the converted data into an existing HTML file.

Click on the first option.

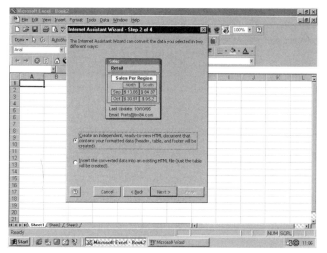

Figure 11.4: The second step in converting data to HTML format

Step 3

At this stage of the operation, you must design your Web page, completing the Title, Header and Description below header. Your converted data are shown.

The Wizard asks you to type in the document's page header or footer, if you want to.

Step 4

At this stage you must indicate the code page, name and location of the completed Web page.

The Wizard asks you what code page to use for your Web page. You are offered a default reply: 'US/Western European'. You could have put: 'Japan'. The access path of your document in HTML format is specified.

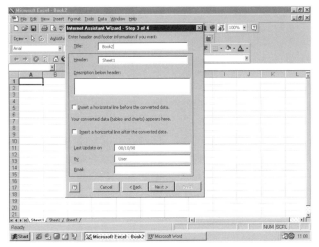

Figure 11.5: Step 3: type your document's title and header

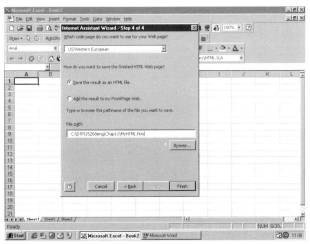

Figure 11.6: The access path of your document in HTML format is now specified

DISPLAYING A WEB PAGE USING NETSCAPE NAVIGATOR

Netscape is the most widely used navigator. Alone it represents 80% of the market. This software makes it possible to read the pages of the World Wide Web and to move from one to another via hyperlinks.

The reasons for the success of Netscape Navigator are its ease of use and the fact that it is free of charge.

Its main competitor, Microsoft Internet Explorer, uses the same principle. Its relative success is a result of the fact that it arrived on the market later.

You want to edit the Euro Fly workbook from the Internet.

You must convert your Euro Fly.xls file into an HTML file.

Proceed as follows:

1. Click on file.

2. Select Save as HTML.

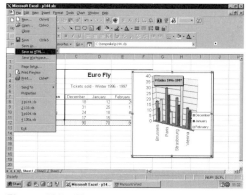

Figure 11.7: To convert your xls file into HTML format, select the Save as HTML option from the File menu

The Internet Assistant Wizard opens during the first stage of the operation. It asks you to specify the range of the spreadsheet to be converted to HTML format.

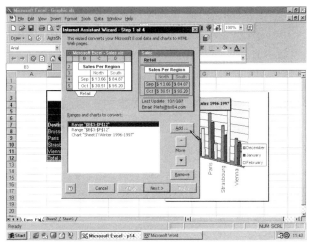

Figure 11.8: The range of the spreadsheet to be converted to an HTML file

1. Click on Next, which gives you access to the second step.

2. Repeat the operation as far as the fourth step.

3. Your xls file is now converted to an HTML file.

The Internet Assistant Wizard at this stage indicates the file path of your spreadsheet which has been converted into an HTML file.

All you have to do now is to search for this file.

The mere fact of clicking on it to select it starts Netscape Navigator.

Your Euro Fly workbook opens on the Internet.

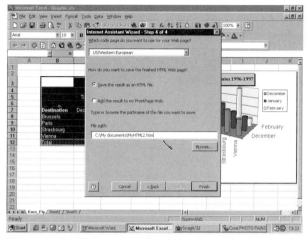

Figure 11.9: During stage four, the file path of your xls file converted into an HTML file appears

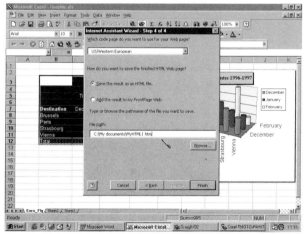

Figure 11.10: Your Euro Fly workbook opens on the Internet

CREATING A HYPERLINK

▰▰▰▰ What is a hyperlink?

A hyperlink makes it possible to link data which may be of different types, for example text to graphic, and vice versa. It offers a shortcut which enables fast access to other folders and files. Using this method, you can access files on your computer or on the World Wide Web.

In order to move from one folder to another, just click on a link (the address) which appears underlined and in blue. When consultation of the file is completed, this link changes from blue to violet.

▰▰▰▰ Creating a hyperlink

Let us imagine that you want to create a hyperlink to a Word document in a spreadsheet.

Open the Euro Fly spreadsheet and the Word document to which you want to link it ('Christmas in Strasbourg').

1. Select the entire Word document 'Christmas in Strasbourg'.

2. Click on Edit and select the Copy submenu.

3. Activate the Excel Euro Fly document.

4. Click on the cell which is to contain the hyperlink: for our example, this is the destination 'Strasbourg' of your Euro Fly table.

5. Click on Edit.

6. Select the paste submenu as hyperlink.

7. Confirm by clicking on OK.

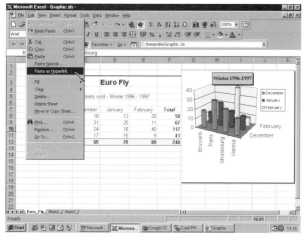

Figure 11.11: Select the Paste as Hyperlink option from the Edit menu

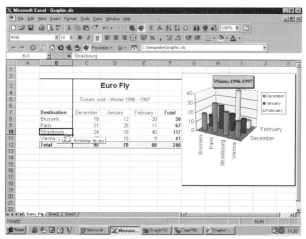

Figure 11.12: Click on the link when your cursor turns into a small white hand

You will notice that the text which you previously selected appears in the cell containing the link.

The word 'Strasbourg' is written in blue.

To activate the text 'Christmas in Strasbourg' to which it refers, just click on this link when the cursor turns into a small white hand.

When you have finished your consultation, the Strasbourg hyperlink will appear in violet.

NAVIGATING ON THE WEB

To navigate on the Web you must have a modem which will connect you with your service provider's server. Once this connection has been established, just start your search by typing the address of the site that you want to visit in your Internet navigator.

 To visit a site, whose address [Uniform Resource Locator(URL)] you know, using Excel 97, click on Go on the Web toolbar and select Open.

Figure 11.13: The Open option of the Go menu

Then enter the address of the site that you want to visit.

You thus arrive at the Web site whose address you have entered.

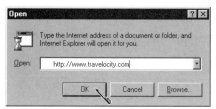

Figure 11.14: Type the address of the Internet site that you want to visit

OPENING FAVORITES

You are surfing the Web, you like a site and you 'bookmark' it to add it to the list of your favourite sites. When you want to go there next time, you just have to click on the Favorites menu and select the Open Favorites submenu.

Figure 11.15: Select the option Open Favorites from the Favorites menu

The Favorites dialog box will appear on screen and you will select the site SDV-Summary, for example.

Your site is now part of the list of favourites. Whenever you want to go there, just drop down the Favorites menu and click on it.

GOING TO THE START PAGE

The Start Page icon starts the default Internet connection routine which you have set up in Internet Explorer. The Internet screen appears on the Excel 97 background, as for a normal session. The start page is the first page displayed in Explorer. It contains instructions concerning using the Web and hyperlinks.

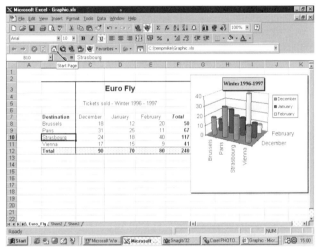

Figure 11.16: The Start Page icon

You can specify another start page at any time:

1. Drop down the Go menu.

2. Click on the Choose a start page icon.

The Start Page dialog box displays the start page's file path.

PUTTING URLS IN THE SPREADSHEET

To create a hyperlink from your spreadsheet:

1. Click in the box where you want to show your Internet address, called an URL (Uniform Resource Locator).

2. Click on Insert.

3. Select the Hyperlink option.

Figure 11.17: The Hyperlink option of the Insert menu

1. Type your address in the text box.

2. Click on Run.

3. Indicate the file to which you want this Internet address to be linked.

4. Confirm by clicking on OK.

Your URL is inserted in the selected spreadsheet. It is in blue to differentiate it from the other data.

Just click on it when your cursor turns into a small white hand and the associated site appears on screen.

Hour 12

Printing the spreadsheet

THE CONTENTS FOR THIS HOUR

- Using Print Preview
- Defining a print area
- Changing the page orientation
- Repeating titles on every page
- Centring on the page
- Printing gridlines
- Printing in black and white
- Printing comments
- Printing a spreadsheet on several pages
- Printing several workbooks simultaneously

- Printing a graph

- Printing a specific area in a spreadsheet

- Adding headers and footers

- Printing the spreadsheet

- Selecting another printer

By default, Excel prints the whole of the spreadsheet unless otherwise specified. To print a limited area of the spreadsheet, you must select it. The software has efficient formatting commands which you access via the Page Setup option of the File menu.

Depending on the printer which is configured, the available parameters are as follows:

Page

- **Orientation:** the spreadsheet may be printed in Portrait (i.e. vertically) or in Landscape (i.e. horizontally).

- **Paper size:** this option gives instructions concerning the paper size.

- **Scaling:** this scales (enlarges or reduces) the spreadsheet so that it prints as a fraction of its original size.

- **Adjust to:** this carries out an automatic calculation of the coefficient of reduction in order to fit the document onto a given number of pages.

Margins

- **Define:** this relates to the top, bottom, left and right margins.

Ensure that the margins defined are in keeping with the page headers and footers.

- **Center on page:** this centres the document in terms of height and/or width.

- **Row and column numbers:** this states whether or not row and column numbers are to be printed.

- **Gridlines:** this states whether or not gridlines are to be printed. This option does not affect what is displayed on screen.

- **Size:** this option basically concerns graphics.

USING PRINT PREVIEW

To print your Euro Fly chart, start by previewing your spreadsheet. This function enables you to preview the final presentation of your document.

1. Click on the File menu.

2. Select Print Preview.

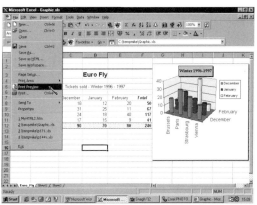

Figure 12.1: Selecting the Print Preview option

The preview screen appears with the information concerning margins, pages, page breaks and zoom.

Zoom

Once your spreadsheet is previewed, your cursor becomes a small magnifying glass. Click and your spreadsheet changes from full page to maximised. This temporary change does not affect the print size. You can switch between displays by clicking on any area and returning to Print Preview mode.

Figure 12.2: Zoom enables you to change to maximised display

You have placed the magnifying glass on the chart. Zoom enables you to see all the details.

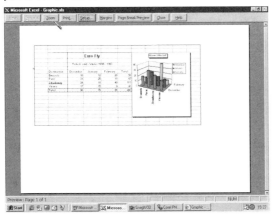

Figure 12.3: The zoom button in Print Preview

186

Margins

By clicking on the margins tab you activate the spreadsheet's margins and they will appear on screen.

You can adjust them by dragging your cursor, which then becomes two black arrows, one horizontal and the other vertical.

Figure 12.4: The margin resizing arrows

DEFINING A PRINT AREA

Using the Set Print Area

Let us suppose that you only want to print the chart and not the graphic. Select your chart and click on the Set Print Area icon.

Then click on the Print icon or the Print option of the File menu.

Only your chart will be printed.

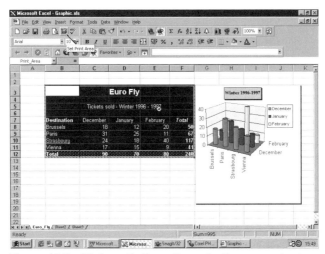

Figure 12.5: Click on Define after selecting your chart

Using the menu

To define a print area using the menu:

1. Select your chart.

2. Click on the File menu.

3. Click on the Print Area option.

4. Select Define.

Only your chart is printed.

To deselect your print area:

1. Click on the File menu.

2. Select the Print Area option.

3. Click on Cancel.

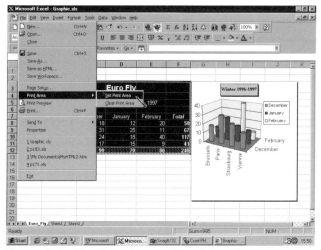

Figure 12.6: The Print Area option of the File menu

CHANGING THE PAGE ORIENTATION

Perhaps you feel that your chart is not the right way round once it is printed. It has come out 'portrait' (vertical) and you would prefer it 'landscape' (horizontal).

To do this:

1. Select your chart.

2. Click on Define.

3. Click on File.

4. Select the Page Setup option and check the Landscape box.

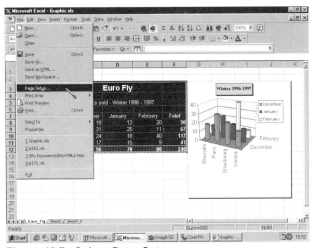

Figure 12.7: Select Page Setup

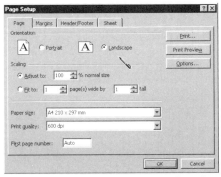

Figure 12.8: The Landscape option: Page tab of the Page Setup dialog box

REPEATING TITLES ON EVERY PAGE

If you have column or row titles, you may want to print them on every page of your spreadsheet.

1. In the File menu, select the Page Setup option.

2. Click on the Sheet tab.

3. In the Print titles text box, specify those which you want to appear at the top of rows and left of columns.

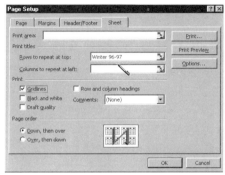

Figure 12.9: Select the Print titles option

CENTRING ON THE PAGE

1. Click on the Margins tab.

2. Check the Horizontally and Vertically boxes of the Center on page option.

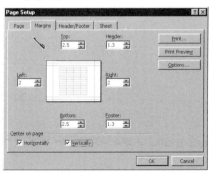

Figure 12.10: The Margins tab and its value counters

PRINTING GRIDLINES

1. Click on the File menu.

2. Select the Page Setup option.

3. Click on the Sheet tab.

4. Check the Gridlines option in the Print area.

PRINTING IN BLACK AND WHITE

If you have formatted data in colour (underlining, text, graph or border) and you have only a black and white printer:

1. Click on the File menu.

2. Select the Page Setup option.

3. Click on the Sheet tab.

4. Check the Black and white box in the Print area.

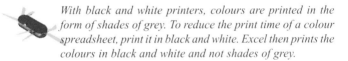

With black and white printers, colours are printed in the form of shades of grey. To reduce the print time of a colour spreadsheet, print it in black and white. Excel then prints the colours in black and white and not shades of grey.

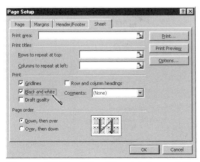

Figure 12.11: The Sheet tab and its Black and white option

PRINTING COMMENTS

At the end of the spreadsheet

If you want to print your spreadsheet with comments:

1. Click on the File menu.

2. Select the Page Setup option.

3. Click on the Sheet tab.

4. Select At end of sheet in the Comments text box.

As displayed on sheet

If you want to print the comments as they appear in the spreadsheet:

1. Click on the File menu.

2. Select the Page Setup option.

3. Click on the Sheet tab.

4. Select 'As displayed on sheet' in the Comments: text box.

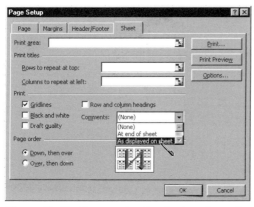

Figure 12.12: Comments: As displayed on sheet, under the Sheet tab

Excel 97

PRINTING A SPREADSHEET ON SEVERAL PAGES

To print your spreadsheet on several pages:

1. Click on the File menu.
2. Select the Page Setup option.
3. Click on the Page tab.
4. Check the Fit to box.
5. Specify the print width and height in terms of number of pages.

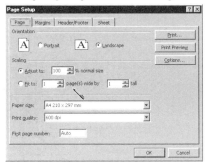

Figure 12.13: Checking the Fit to box

PRINTING SEVERAL WORKBOOKS SIMULTANEOUSLY

1. Select Open from the File menu.
2. Hold the Ctrl key down and click on all the workbooks that you want to print.
3. Click on the Commands and Settings icon.
4. Print.

194

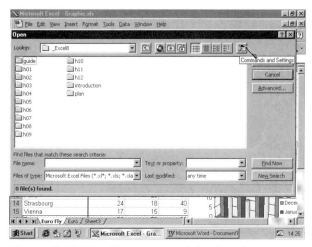

Figure 12.14: The Commands and Settings icon

PRINTING A GRAPH

Graph on a graphic worksheet

To print a graph on a graphic worksheet, just scale it at the time of printing.

1. Activate the graphic worksheet.

2. Click on the File menu.

3. Select the Page Setup option.

4. Click on the Graph tab.

5. In the Size of printed graph box, click on the desired scaling option.

6. If you click on the Customize option, the graph will be printed at the size that you have defined yourself.

▬▬▬ Graph embedded in a spreadsheet

If your graph is embedded in the spreadsheet, you must resize it.

1. Click on the graph.
2. Drag the selection handles to the required size.

If you want to print your embedded graph without the spreadsheet data, click on the graph to select it, click on Page Setup, select the File option and click on the Graph tab.

PRINTING A SPECIFIC AREA IN A SPREADSHEET

To print a specific area in a spreadsheet:

1. Click on View.
2. Select Page Break Preview.
3. Select the area to be printed.
4. Click with the right mouse button on the selected area.
5. Click on Define in the contextual menu.

The contextual menu is the floating menu which is accessed by clicking on an object with the right mouse button.

You can add cells to your print area at any time when in Page Break Preview mode. Just select the cells to be added, click on one of the selected cells using the right mouse button, then select the Add to print area option from the contextual menu.

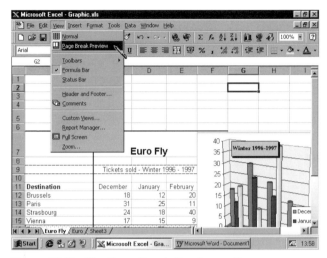

Figure 12.15: The Page Break Preview option

ADDING HEADERS AND FOOTERS

Before printing your chart, you can add a header and a footer. You can select from predefined samples or create your own.

A spreadsheet can take only one header and one footer. If you have created your own, it will automatically replace the default.

Customised headers and footers

Excel offers automatic printing of the date and time. To access this:

1. Click on View.

2. Select the Header and footer option.

3. Select Header.

4. Enter the title of your chart in the Center section. You can choose between Center section, Left section and Right section. You can use all three to enter your names if you wish.

5. By clicking on the Tab, File, Time, Date, Page and Font icons, you can customise your headers and footers.

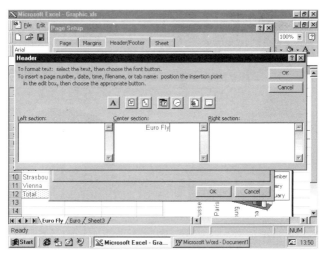

Figure 12.16: A customised header and footer

▬▬▬ Predefined headers and footers

To access the predefined headers and footers:

1. Click on View.

2. Select the Header and Footer option.

3. In the Header/Footer box, select the one which suits you.

PRINTING THE SPREADSHEET

Once all the parameters have been set, print your spreadsheet:

1. Click on File.

2. Select the Print option.

3. Do not forget to specify the number of copies that you want to print.

4. If you are printing more than one, specify whether or not you want the copies collated. If so, check the Collate box.

5. Confirm by clicking on OK.

Printing will then begin.

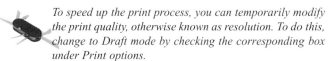

To speed up the print process, you can temporarily modify the print quality, otherwise known as resolution. To do this, change to Draft mode by checking the corresponding box under Print options.

SELECTING ANOTHER PRINTER

If you use more than one printer with your computer, you can easily change from one to another provided that you select the one you want each time.

1. Click on File.

2. Select the Print option.

3. Click on the drop-down list of printers in the Printer box.

4. Select the one you want.

5. Confirm by clicking on OK.

Index

E

Edit
button 164
Effects 63
Entering information
data 25
date form 119
dates 25
numbers 25
time 25

F

Fields 118
File format 35
Filters
AutoFilter 127
Advanced Filter 128
Fitting text 46
Footers
adding 197
customised 197
predefined 198
Fonts 40
size 41
Form
data 119
Format
file 35
financial 27
Formatting
chart 145
AutoFormat 50
printing (Page Setup) 192

Formula 77
copying 78
matrix 84
Function Wizard 83

G

Graphics
copying 56
importing 56
Gridlines
printing 185, 192

H

Header
adding 197
customised 197
predefined 198
Height
row 42
Help
Office Assistant 17

I

Importing graphics 56
Incremented string 88
copying 88
Info-bubbles 11
Installing Excel 97 6
Internet 165

W

Z